ALSO BY BRIN-JONATHAN BUTLER

*The Domino Diaries*

*A Cuban Boxer's Journey*

# THE
# GRANDMASTER

MAGNUS CARLSEN AND THE MATCH
THAT MADE CHESS GREAT AGAIN

BRIN-JONATHAN BUTLER

SIMON & SCHUSTER

NEW YORK   LONDON   TORONTO   SYDNEY   NEW DELHI

Simon & Schuster
1230 Avenue of the Americas
New York, NY 10020

First Simon & Schuster hardcover edition November 2018

SIMON & SCHUSTER and colophon are registered
trademarks of Simon & Schuster, Inc.

For information about special discounts for bulk purchases,
please contact Simon & Schuster Special Sales
at 1-866-506-1949 or business@simonandschuster.com.

The Simon & Schuster Speakers Bureau can bring authors to your live event.
For more information or to book an event, contact the
Simon & Schuster Speakers Bureau at 1-866-248-3049 or
visit our website at www.simonspeakers.com.

*Interior design by Ruth Lee-Mui*

Manufactured in the United States of America

1   3   5   7   9   10   8   6   4   2

Library of Congress Cataloging-in-Publication Data has been applied for.

ISBN 978-1-5011-7260-1
ISBN 978-1-5011-7262-5 (ebook)

*This book is for Vallory Friesen and Glenn Stout.*

"Do you see over yonder, friend Sancho, thirty or forty hulking giants? I intend to do battle with them and slay them."

—Miguel de Cervantes, Don Quixote

# CONTENTS

# THE GRANDMASTER

# 1

# A NIGHT AT THE PLAZA

In AD 813, a fratricidal power struggle and civil war saw Baghdad, the capital of the Islamic empire, buried under a ceaseless hail of rocks, an inferno of burning pots of oil. The Tigris River was aflame with ignited rafts, stained in human blood, and bloated with bodies and sunken boats. After two years of raging civil war between Caliph al-Amīn and his half brother al-Ma'mūn, starved defenders gave up their last ounces of strength desperately trying to reinforce the gates. Urban warfare continued to rage in the streets as the "Naked Army" (mostly amateur troops of African origin comprised of street vendors, market sellers, even inmates from prisons, who went into battle without armor or any kind of body protection) offered the last gasp of the city's defense. As the artillery of catapults flung heavy stones, arrows soared, battering rams and swords crashed, far removed from the action, shielded by an abundance of walls, gates, and imperial guards, and tranquilly sitting beneath the green dome of the Golden Gate Palace, Caliph al-Amīn, the sixth caliph of the Abbāsid dynasty, ignored the overwhelming chaos and onslaught outside his kingdom. Instead, as his various palaces burned into the night, he focused on a chessboard and pondered his next move.

A panicked messenger arrived to impart the news that, having incurred a new series of bitter losses, the caliph's brother might soon win the war. Al-Amīn's life was in dire peril. But the caliph didn't care or even bother to look up from the board.

According to Islamic historian Jirjis al-Makin, the messenger deliriously begged the caliph to stop playing and take stock of his kingdom.

Caliph al-Amīn's attention remained glued to his pieces, their future on the board vastly more optimistic than that of his real troops defending his kingdom. Soon after al-Amīn successfully mated his adversary on the chessboard, his brother's troops arrived and, not too long afterward, the caliph was decapitated. The War of the Two Brothers had concluded.

Eight centuries later and more than twenty-five hundred miles northwest of Baghdad in England, in the winter of 1648, a messenger arrived at the court of King Charles I with dire news. The messenger found the king hopelessly absorbed in a game of chess on his precious amber board. The board had been a gift from his father, King James I. It was built by Georg Schreiber, renowned as the "King of the Gamesboards," in Königsberg in 1607, constructed from preciously small amounts of amber that had washed up onto the shores of the East Sea.

In between moves, Charles read the message. The Scots had betrayed him. He remained seated and gave no indication of the missive's contents to his royal court by any gesture or expression on his face. Instead, he kept playing. The message was tantamount to the king's death warrant, yet the game continued.

When Charles was executed on January 30, 1649—the first English monarch ever to be put to death—he was allowed to carry two belongings with him to the scaffold where he was beheaded: he chose a Bible and his chessboard. A bishop named William Juxon read Charles his last rites atop scaffolding with a hooded executioner looking on. The king's last action before placing his head on the block was to offer the Bible and chessboard to the bishop as a gift.

Jump ahead to the afternoon of November 10, 2016, two days after Donald Trump was elected the forty-fifth president of the United States: thousands swarmed the Trump International Hotel & Tower near Manhattan's Columbus Circle. A mile away, at Trump's Fifth Avenue residence, protesters battered a piñata of the president-elect. Police closed down the avenue at Fifty-Seventh Street and barricaded demonstrators.

I watched one kid nestled inside the mob drop an American flag on the ground while his friend squeezed a stream of lighter fluid over it. Someone else bent over to reach down toward the flag, their Zippo's flame delicately fluttering in the frigid cold, to ignite the bonfire.

That same night, I walked just a few blocks west and joined several hundred invitation-only guests who strolled across a red carpet into the Plaza Hotel's Palm Court. They were almost entirely white and older and, judging by their jet-lagged faces and well-tutored accents, Russian and European. Women in backless dresses milled about, their porcelain skin illuminated under opulent crystal chandeliers. Waiters circulated through the crowd with trays of white and black Russian cocktails and delicately sculptured hors d'oeuvres. A black gospel choir sang "Happy."

This was the opening-night celebration of the World Chess Championship (WCC) between Norway's Magnus Carlsen and Russia's Sergey Karjakin—a best-of-twelve match over two and a half weeks for a grand prize of $1.1 million. If Trump was the glacier and America was the *Titanic*, then the Plaza felt like the unsinkable ship's game room—and the only thing anyone seemed to care about was chess.

This wasn't the first time the Plaza had been a part of chess history. Nearly twenty years before, in the spring of 1997, then world champion Garry Kasparov had rented a suite there to prepare for his rematch against the IBM computer Deep Blue, which he had already beaten the year before. But on this night, during this week, the Plaza's connection to chess was overshadowed by its connection to Trump. When he bought the hotel in 1988, he boasted that he hadn't purchased "a building, I have purchased a masterpiece— the *Mona Lisa*. For the first time in my life, I have knowingly made a deal that was not economic—for I can never justify the price I paid, no matter how successful the Plaza becomes." That price was $407.5 million, equal to roughly twice that amount in today's dollars. The Plaza did not become successful. Four years later it went into bankruptcy. Trump eventually sold it to a Saudi prince and one of Singapore's leading entrepreneurs for $325 million. Before that, though, in 1993, he married his second wife, Marla Maples, in front of more than eleven hundred guests at the Plaza. Also not successful.

That the WCC gala was at a location synonymous with the new president on the very same week as the election was pure coincidence. The venue had been booked months in advance, according to the communications director for Agon Limited, a sports event–promoting company that was founded in New Jersey in 2012. That same year, the company was granted long-term marketing rights to the World Chess Championship by the Fédération Internationale des Échecs, or World Chess Federation (FIDE), the sport's international governing body. Agon's mission was, as stated on their website, "to turn chess into the [*sic*] spectator sport and attractive platform for brand [*sic*] and partners alike."

More than six hundred million people around the world played chess, about the same number as the global population of domestic cats. If chess were a religion, its adherents would make it the fourth largest in existence. Agon was essentially looking to do for chess what had been done for poker in the early 2000s. Tournaments on ESPN. Corporate sponsorship. Revenue from online gambling.

Mirroring Trump's hopes for America, they wanted to make chess great again. What could possibly stand in their way?

So Agon had booked the gala at the Plaza. And, for the first time in the history of the match, the event would be streamed online. The stream would feature multi-camera views and even a 360-degree virtual reality option. It would also feature chess-legend commentators such as Judit Polgár, who in 2005 had achieved the world ranking of eighth, the highest ever for a female player.

Then there was the venue itself, a one-hundred-thousand-square-foot space located in the Fulton Market Building in Lower

Manhattan. Nearly one hundred workers had been hired to customize the interior, which included a broadcast studio; viewing areas; playing areas; a café; a separate VIP area with a bar; and the soundproof, glassed-in cube where Carlsen and Karjakin would face off.

Agon had invested roughly $5 million in the event. They were hoping for about a thousand attendees per day. Tickets were $75 per day—$1,200 for the VIP area. To stream the event cost $15 for the entire match, or $1.25 per game.

But, as with any event in America, it wasn't anything unless there was a celebrity presence. There was certainly no shortage of famous chess fans. Bill Gates. Mark Zuckerberg. Peter Thiel. Zuckerberg and Gates were reported in one paper as possibly attending. And so, for the gala's emcee, Agon hired none other than . . . Adrian Grenier, the star of HBO's *Entourage*, which had run from 2004 until 2011. Clearly the most intuitive choice.

Nobody seemed quite sure what Grenier had to do with chess, but from the limited understanding I had of his work, Grenier gave one of the peak performances of his career as he regaled the audience with chess factoids he read from handheld cue cards and made lame jokes about chess's superiority to apps like *Candy Crush Saga* and *Angry Birds*. Someone behind me whispered that he'd been paid six figures for showing up. After his speech, he stood for photos with Carlsen and Karjakin. They looked just as confused about who he was and why he was there.

But what about me? There was a reasonable question to address before long: What the hell was *I* doing there?

A week before, I'd gotten a Twitter DM from an editor at Simon & Schuster. He wanted someone to write a book about Magnus

Carlsen, a book that tried to answer three questions. One: Why wasn't the dude more of a household name? Here was a guy who had been the top-ranked chess player in the world for the past six years and had the highest rating of any chess player in history—higher than Kasparov and Bobby Fischer. Yet Kasparov and Fischer—not Carlsen—were still the names that most non-chess people thought of when they thought about chess. It was like Carlsen was Roger Federer and everybody was still talking about Andre Agassi and Pete Sampras. Two: What was the secret to his greatness? How exactly had he managed to be so much better than everyone else for so long? At least Federer had a true rival in Rafael Nadal, whereas nobody had come close to challenging Carlsen for supremacy. And, finally, three: How long could he continue to do it? More specifically, given the fierce pressures, how long could he continue to do it without cracking the way Fischer and a surprising number of other chess champions had? How did the pressures and stress of staying on top affect Carlsen with all the top players in the world gunning for his crown?

The editor thought I'd be especially suited to try and answer these questions, because I'd made a career from writing about characters on the outer margins of the sports world. Mostly boxers, bullfighters, and controversial high-profile athletes. I had written two books about Cuba, exploring the country through the prism of its greatest boxers, who were used as political pawns by Fidel Castro, and had spent time with and profiled many of the biggest names in the sport in America. My journalism career began on Easter Sunday of 2010, by accident, when I managed to find a way into Mike Tyson's Las Vegas residence. Through a thick haze of weed smoke, I was initially greeted by Tyson with, "So how did this white motherfucker get inside my house?" I'd also written about the Spanish bullfighter José Tomás and the New York Yankees pitcher El Duque and his escape from Cuba. Lance Armstrong once approached me with the prospect of ghostwriting his tell-all memoir: "It's a mix of *Raging Bull*, *Chariots of Fire*, and *Brian's Song*," Lance explained, laughing, when we met at the bar of the Mandarin Oriental hotel in New York to discuss the project. "It's complicated. It's dirty. But would we do it any different?"

So yeah: I had a thing for people living lives at the extremes of what they did and trying to find unusual angles on what made them tick. On that level, I could see why the editor thought of me. But what he didn't know was that, though I had never written about chess, I had a very deep and strange personal connection to the game—an obsession I'd suppressed and had only very recently been reminded of.

It was the summer of 1998: my nineteenth birthday was around the corner, and I had just been dumped by my first girlfriend. She was my first kiss and we'd been together for over two years, spending half of that time sharing an apartment in Vancouver, where I grew up. Somehow I'd imagined my first girlfriend was going to be my last girlfriend and we'd be together the rest of our lives. My father's parents had done that. But that didn't work out for me and I took it very hard and booked a one-way flight from Vancouver to Europe. I spent my first month backpacking around Europe, basically undergoing a prolonged nervous breakdown. I blew through more money on long-distance phone calls back to my ex than on traveling. I visited many of the capital cities of Europe—London, Paris, Madrid, Brussels, Amsterdam, Berlin—and an hour after arriving in each, I'd only move into another cold foreign phone booth and call another operator. Instead of helping, each call only made my situation worse and pushed her farther away.

I'd flunked out of high school the previous year, but my father had offered me the mitzvah of the money he'd saved up for my college. He'd had his first heartbreak at the same age as me, and when I asked him at the airport why he trusted me with the money, since I'd let him down with school, he smiled for a long time before he replied.

"You don't trust the world because it's trustworthy," he said. "You trust the world because not trusting is a guarantee that your life will end up without anything worthwhile that the world has to offer. I trust you, and I trust the path you're going to find in the world."

But in Europe I was screwing that all up too. With each country I visited, I had one less place in the world that might offer a sanctuary or at least foxhole from what I was running from. So I finally tried my mother's family in Budapest, whom I'd never met.

My grandfather had left the country during the Hungarian Revolution of 1956, when my uncle was eight and my mother only six. He entered Canada as a refugee and immediately started working. It took him ten years to raise enough money to bring his family over. By then it was too late for my grandmother and uncle. Their lives were in Budapest and they no longer wished to leave, but my sixteen-year-old mother chose to join him. Unfortunately, she didn't reunite with the father who'd left ten years earlier. He was someone horribly different.

After my grandmother had divorced my grandfather, a few months before my mother came over to Canada, he'd fallen in love with an engaged Hungarian woman who had also left the country in 1956. When this woman told him in no uncertain terms his feelings were severely unrequited, he took revenge and hanged himself from a balcony in front of her and her fiancé during a New Year's party. His fellow partygoers were able to cut him down, but the lack of air to his brain left him in a coma for the next fifty-six days. He woke up with an entirely different personality—cold, bitter, violent.

By the age of seventeen, my mother had run away from her father's home and dropped out of high school, getting married and becoming pregnant within a year. After giving birth to a son, she lost her next child to crib death. Three years later she had an affair and gave birth to my other brother, which led to a divorce and her raising both of her sons in Vancouver's low-income housing projects while she worked odd menial jobs to put food on the table. My mom met my dad just before he finished law school and started his own child protection private law practice. I was born the year after that, in 1979. My father bought the family a house and was almost immediately forced to sell it for a huge loss when the real estate market crashed. He was buried in debt and my mother went back to work part-time.

One of her jobs was helping the owner of an antique shop. The first time I stepped inside I was four years old, and I instantly cased the inventory for the most precious treasure on display, zeroing in on the chessboard in the backroom office. It stood out like a sphinx. From a distance, it looked like any of the enticing board games my grandparents had stuffed away in the cupboard: Monopoly, Scrabble, Risk, Sorry, Snakes and Ladders, the Game of Life, Trouble.

The shop's elderly owner left the back room to greet me, but stopped suddenly when he recognized the look on my face as I stared at his chessboard.

"Do you know how to play?" he asked.

I shook my head.

"Don't be afraid," he said gently. "Come a little closer."

As I started over toward him, I noticed he had a glass eye. He offered a strange little smile and asked if I was *sure* I wanted him to teach me how to play chess.

I didn't know what to say. The way he said it almost sounded like a warning, like his board or the game itself was cursed. That he treated chess like some kind of unlocked liquor cabinet only intrigued me more.

I nodded my head.

"Just be a little careful," he warned, with a barely contained gleam in his good eye. "It might never let you go."

And then he beat me in two moves in what's known as a Fool's Mate.

It felt different than losing at all those other board games. It *hurt*. And because I couldn't understand why exactly it hurt so much, it frightened me enormously. I kept my distance over the years. Whenever anybody innocently brought out a chessboard and wanted to play, I'd say no. My feelings about the game weren't unlike my lifelong cautious attitude toward alcohol, which I'd assumed after learning its effect on several members of my family— up close with my dad, and secondhand from my mother, who'd described alcoholism in her family back in Hungary.

But then I arrived in Budapest on the morning of my nineteenth birthday.

• • •

My uncle Bandi was supposed to pick me up at the Nyugati train station—a breathtaking symphony of stone, steel, and glass. My mother hadn't been back since I was a baby, and I think the most recent picture I'd seen of my uncle was an army photo from his mandatory military service. In the black-and-white photograph, he looked like Robert De Niro in *The Godfather Part II*. After I'd spent twenty-five minutes frantically searching for him at the station, a stranger sitting at the bar broke out laughing. In my confusion, it took me a few minutes to identify who the man was. He looked like De Niro if De Niro had packed on a lot of weight to play the part of a corrupt, small-town Hungarian cop.

My uncle didn't own a car, so he took me on a walking tour of Budapest, which included throwing back a *Leaving Las Vegas* quantity of alcohol. There were pubs on nearly every street—all crammed full with Hungarian men and women from seven in the morning onward—and each hour he'd drink a glass of *fröccs* (white wine and soda) and two shots of something called *pálinka* (famous for being unmixable) and expected me to do the same. It was fairly obvious that Bandi had consumed alcohol at this kind of frightening pace for decades. No matter how much I watched him drink, he gave no indication that it had any effect on him.

Bandi had an ex-wife, a daughter, and a handful of girlfriends. They all lived in close proximity to one another and, somehow, were friends. We drank at all their apartments too. Because of my family history, that day was the first time I had ever touched alcohol. I was expected to keep up drinking with my hardened alcoholic uncle and was anesthetized after two hours and nearly blackout drunk by lunchtime. Since the Hungarian Revolution, Hungary had one of the highest suicide rates in the world, and for a while it just seemed like my uncle and I were bonding while doing our part to fit in.

Bandi spoke no English, yet he worked furiously over a Hungarian-English dictionary to explain the sights and history of Budapest. Before we got to that, he kindly informed me that my mother was a Gypsy (it was abundantly clear Bandi's attitude to the Romani population in Budapest was buoyantly genocidal) and, given my darker complexion, had cheated on my father with a black man (he used the other hateful word). Presumably to help make me feel at home, when we encountered anyone he knew on the street, Bandi made sure to gleefully introduce me as his nephew, *the bastard son of his sister from a black man.*

As we passed the Danube, I was told that the Scourge of God, Attila the Hun, had been placed in a triple-layered coffin of gold, silver, and lead and buried in an unknown, dammed-off portion of the Tisza River. When they let the river flow over the grave, anyone who had witnessed the burial and knew the location was killed or blinded with nails driven into their eyes. He showed me the gorgeous Erzsébet Bridge, which shared my mother's name and had been built only two years before she left the country. Near Heroes' Square, he led me to a park where I was introduced to the ominous statue of what appeared to be the Grim Reaper, but was in fact the statue of Anonymous, an ancient Hungarian king's chronicler, holding a shiny pen. The legend was that if you touched the pen you would become a great writer. He'd heard from my mother that I wanted to be a writer and used the dictionary to communicate to me that I needed all the luck I could get.

When I tried to order a round of beer, I was warned that the 150-year statute of limitations on clinking glasses wasn't up yet.

Apparently, in 1848, when the Hungarian Revolution against the Habsburgs was defeated, thirteen Hungarian generals were put to death. Legend had it that after each execution of a general, the Austrians clinked their glasses to celebrate. A Hungarian prohibition was enacted on beer-glass clinking for 150 years to honor the memory of the generals.

That's the last detail I remember from the Budapest tour before everything got blurry and the nausea really set in.

Bandi took me back to the apartment where he had grown up with my mother in Pest, the eastern region of the city, which was flat compared to Buda, with its hills and fortress. I remember an almost Gothic staircase that swung along an enormous curve to my grandmother's door. My grandmother stood behind the door, dressed entirely in black, mourning the recent death of her beloved second husband. She was holding a little passport photo of him in her hand. She talked to it. She talked to me in French to try to bridge the language gap despite my not speaking any French. My uncle mocked her, and while I barely understood Hungarian, whatever she said sounded like she was reminding him for the thousandth time that she wished he'd never been born. My uncle dug a finger into her armpit until she swatted it away. They had a scary dance between them.

Bandi took us into a back room and showed us the family chessboard.

"My fadder," he said gently—departing from his usual growl—before reaching into his Hungarian-English dictionary for assistance. "Teach . . . me . . . chezz . . . theez . . . board . . . when . . . child."

When Bandi's daughter Zsuzsi came over to visit our

grandmother later that day, it turned out she was a gifted linguist in many languages and conversational in English. She told me that learning chess from his father was one of Bandi's last and most cherished childhood memories of the man.

Later that night, Bandi took me to a run-down, cavernous bar near the Danube, bringing the family chessboard along with him. A tiny girl with ribbons in her hair, who was sitting next to her mother at the piano, began playing a haunting little melody on her own. Some years later, I finally identified it as the middle of Béla Bartók's *Román Népi Táncok*. Her fingers delicately scampered across the piano keys like the paws of a cat leaving footprints in the snow as it scampered over the gravestones inside a cemetery.

My uncle reached into a leather satchel and produced his ornate but battered chessboard and a Wonka-purple velvet pouch tied with a yellow string and full of deformed wooden pieces. The loser, he informed me, was to pick up the bar tab. But my uncle's smile and the glint in his black eyes suggested something more was on the line. I immediately remembered the antique shop owner's warning about chess, but was too drunk to follow it. And Bandi's wasn't exactly the most sympathetic ear in which to enter a protest against playing, so I gave in.

I lost every game to him inside that bar. He was a sadist over the chessboard, never finding more delight than in pinning my pieces as he closed in for the slaughter. Before it was over, I threw up in the bathroom. He carried me home to my grandmother's apartment. Once I got there, I horrified my grandmother by throwing up all over everything; the next day, in my mother's old bed, I nursed the first and most egregious hangover of my life. After cleaning up the mess, I went back to the Nyugati train station and took the first train out to Prague. I never saw my grandmother or uncle again.

A strange thing happened after I arrived in Prague. For hours I searched all over the city for a place to stay but couldn't find anything. Nothing was available. I went back to the train station late at night with nowhere else to go. Looking at the unsavory characters milling around, I realized that it was far from safe to sleep there. Only one Czech shop was open at the train station and, interestingly enough, it sold knives. I was eyeing a switchblade when I noticed they also sold travel chess sets. So I bought one of each for the remainder of my journey.

By the time I got home a month later, I was completely hooked on the game. For the next two years, I basically *lived* in cafés and always brought a chessboard along to entice other chess addicts. I bought a clock, and bullet chess—a game played with only one minute for each player—became my duel of choice. I gave up writing and spent the summers hustling tourists for money outside the Vancouver Art Gallery—my hometown's answer to New York's Washington Square Park—every afternoon until dark. I don't think I ever earned more than fifty bucks in a day, and if anyone of any real strength at chess passed through, I was demolished. But it didn't matter. An alcoholic isn't especially encouraged to give up drinking after encountering someone who can hold their liquor better than he can.

It's not an accident that chess has been one of the most durable things humanity has created in the last fifteen hundred years. Think of all the precious, cherished things people have lost in that time along the way to the present: languages, religions, civilizations, entire bloodlines, endless artifacts, and countless stories cast into a common darkness. How did something so seemingly trivial as chess prove so much more durable and immune to the friction and chaos of history? Any child can learn the basics in minutes, yet no human mind will ever be capable of solving it any more than an abacus has a prayer of measuring a black hole.

But then I got hooked on something even less practical, writing a novel, and found it was impossible to do both. One poisoned the well you drank from for the other. I went back to writing and gave away my board and clock.

My grandmother died a few years later, and my uncle moved into her apartment and quit his job to finally devote himself to drinking with unfettered dedication. Ten years after I saw him, he acquired diabetes and both his legs had to be amputated below the knee. His liver began to give out, but he still drank in his wheelchair.

By October 2016, Bandi was in the hospital. He asked my mother to fly back to Budapest to visit him one final time to say goodbye. She had returned only a few times as an adult, the last time to see her mother shortly before my grandmother's death. She called and told me Bandi had still found ways to smuggle liquor into the hospital room and had only given it up after they started administering morphine.

When my mother returned to Canada, she mentioned that Bandi had given her a package to send to me in New York and that he had asked her not to open it. On Halloween, the package arrived outside my door in the eight-story walk-up where I live on 110th Street in Spanish Harlem. My building's stoop was decked out in cobweb and skeleton decorations and Hillary Clinton signs. Most of the families who lived in my building were of Mexican descent, and they hadn't taken kindly to Trump calling them criminals and rapists. All the families I knew in my building were working their asses off just to stay afloat in the city.

So was I. The books about Cuba hadn't sold, and before I could discuss ideas for another with my editor, he died from a heroin overdose at the age of twenty-seven. I was barely making ends meet freelancing stories, and had turned to giving private boxing lessons. Renting space in a gym was too expensive, so I ran a sort of guerilla operation teaching in Central Park or in my students' living rooms.

I brought the package up to my apartment on the fifth floor and placed it on the windowsill beside my desk. It took me a few days to work up the nerve to open it. Bandi was a rotten human being. I had no idea what perverse item he'd bequeathed to me. Finally I took the package down from my windowsill. Inside was the family chessboard with the Wonka-purple velvet pouch full of pieces. No note. No explanation. My mother euphemistically calls gestures like this Hungarian Jokes. I put the box back on the windowsill, listened to Bartók's *Román Népi Táncok* for several hours on repeat, and started laughing until I cried.

Less than a week later, the Simon & Schuster editor hit me up on Twitter. For a moment, before I realized the DM was legitimate, I thought it was something like publishing's answer to a Nigerian-prince scam.

The editor had been in touch with Agon Limited. He'd told them about the project, and they'd agreed to give me press credentials for both the match and the Plaza gala. They couldn't promise me any one-on-one interview time with Carlsen. I figured at some point I'd be able to finagle some private time with him. I'd talked my way into Tyson's crib—how hard could gaining access to a chess champion be by comparison? But it definitely wasn't happening that night. Several journalists tried unsuccessfully to engage Carlsen, but he only exchanged a few words with some of the chess-beat writers with whom he'd become familiar over the years. But even to their questions he responded with little more than a shrug or a nod. *This is the Roger Federer of his sport?* I thought. *The LeBron James? The Tiger Woods?*

That was certainly the story his PR team and the overlords of chess were trying to sell—or so I'd gathered from the research I'd furiously done on Carlsen in the days since receiving the assignment. Here was something new: not your stereotypical social outcast chess champion—a young, hip chess champion. He had modeled alongside actress Liv Tyler in an advertising campaign for the denim company G-Star Raw. He had appeared in a Porsche commercial with Maria Sharapova and the digitally manipulated ghost of Muhammad Ali. Porsche's ad agency's chief creative officer described Carlsen as "kind of Drake meets Dalai Lama: confident and cool, with the understanding of a universe that you don't know about." In a 2013 article, *Time* had called him "the World's Sexiest Chess Player" and the game's "first sex symbol," specifically citing his "smoldering good looks and six-pack abs." He was spotted with Jay-Z at a Brooklyn Nets game, appeared in an internet video with *The Office* star Rainn Wilson, and checkmated Bill Gates in twelve seconds on late-night Norwegian TV.

But it all felt like staged performance art. While Carlsen smiled for photo ops and a few handshakes with VIPs, he cast his own version of a thousand-yard-stare. You could feel him retreating from the world to somewhere far behind his deep ridge of a brow. He'd look at the ceiling or the ground and something would trigger little trenches of concentration on his face that made him look half like a baby and half like an old man. Only his body was in the Plaza. His mind and imagination were playing over a chess opening or combing one of hundreds of thousands of games in his memory bank for some new glimmer of understanding.

That's not to say Carlsen didn't cast a spell. He absolutely did. But it had very little to do with his physical appearance or outward personality. Instead, there was something behind that stare, something that communicated the vast distance between him and everyone else around him. By accident, he locked eyes with me for a split second, and I had the unsettling yet magical feeling of looking at images beamed from the surface of a remote planet in our solar system via satellite. Maybe some of the metaphysical thrill of chess at the highest level owes something to that quality of transmission. And this twenty-five-year-old kid, like those satellites taking the pictures, was still out there, moving through his own inner space, only in Carlsen's case he was pulled ever further toward his life's passion by a unique form of magnetism.

I had never felt farther away from a human being who was only twenty feet away from me.

As the evening came to a close, I noticed some abandoned chessboards arranged on tables overlooking the Grand Ballroom dance floor and wandered up the stairs toward them. At one of the tables sat a bespectacled, well-dressed American in his mid-twenties—one of the few Americans there, it seemed, besides myself and *Entourage*'s Vinnie Chase. He invited me to sit with him. As we both looked down at Carlsen being photographed with a sponsor, the man turned to me and shrugged. "What if I gave my life to chess? I've thought about it occasionally. But I was a little different. I loved chess, but not *only* chess."

This was an American grandmaster named Robert Hess II. He was a year younger than Carlsen and, at his peak in 2012, age twenty, was ranked fifth in the United States. By the time he was in tenth grade at New York's Stuyvesant High School, Hess had been offered an internship at a hedge fund. Wall Street took notice of him, and Goldman Sachs reached out for meetings around the time Hess achieved the rank of grandmaster, shortly before his eighteenth birthday. Hess went to Yale instead and majored in history. Today he coaches the US Women's Chess Team.

"Personally, what was required at the highest level pushed me away," Hess told me. "It churns out a lot of one-dimensional people. A lot of these top players devote themselves so fully to chess they don't graduate high school. How many of the fifteen hundred or so GMs have a degree? It's a very small percentage. I never wanted to be like that. I always felt different because I enjoyed other things besides chess. I wouldn't have been happy living a professional chess player's lifestyle. Unlike a lot of chess parents, mine were established. I was able to choose."

"Do you wonder how good you could have been if you'd given chess all your life?" I asked.

"Listen . . ." Hess sighed. "Unlike music, chess is about *winning*, not *sharing*. There's nothing worse in life—obviously health issues, family issues, political—but there are very few things worse in this world that have devastated me like losing at chess. The complete objectivity of losing to someone and not some*thing*. You beat yourself up for hours. It's entirely your fault in a way that almost nothing else in life is. And it eats and weighs on you. Chess is a very dangerous parasite. Championship chess is studying for the SAT and taking it for six hours a day and then repeating that over and over."

I had told him about my assignment—how I'd been tasked with figuring out the secret to Carlsen's greatness and ultimately how sustainable it was.

"Do you think for Magnus the sacrifice was worth it?" I asked.

Hess shrugged.

"Is he the best player ever?" I asked.

Hess smiled.

"According to the ratings. But my high school physics teacher, objectively speaking, is better than Isaac Newton ever was at physics. It doesn't necessarily mean he's more *talented*."

# 2

# THE PRODIGIES

Magnus Carlsen, the second of four children, was born on November 30, 1990, to Henrik and Sigrun Carlsen in the town of Tønsberg (population forty thousand), an hour south of Norway's capital. Carlsen's father was a supply manager for Exxon and his mother a chemical engineer. Tønsberg is the oldest town in the land of the midnight sun, with a dramatic seascape and origins so remote few meaningful remnants remain intact. North of the city center lie the ruins of Slottsfjellet (Castle Rock Fort), a majestic fortress dating back to the twelfth century, which burned down in 1503. The annual Tønsberg Medieval Festival features a Grand Parade in which Vikings, knights, and shamans march. Beyond the Viking-era ruins linking the city to its past, just outside Tønsberg is the location where the Berg concentration camp was built during World War II while the Germans occupied Norway. The Berg camp was unique among camps in Norway in that it was run exclusively by collaborating Norwegians.

When Magnus was five years old, his father introduced him to chess. Henrik had been a decent tournament chess player himself and had realized the year before that his son might be good at the game, when Magnus became fixated on books with the flags of the world's countries, capitals, and municipalities. He memorized them all, along with their populations and sizes. His powers of concentration and obsession, even at that age, were such that Henrik had to demand he take breaks in order to eat. He would often observe his son in his bedroom, staring at the ceiling as he processed his assimilated information.

Magnus's obsession with geography wasn't limited to books. "Magnus was always climbing mountains," Ellen Carlsen, the eldest of Magnus's three sisters, said of her famous brother in the 2016 documentary *Magnus*, directed by Benjamin Ree. "And he did climb some really, really tall mountains when he was quite young. I think he learned early that it takes a lot to reach your goals, and he would walk like for ten to twelve hours when he was young." In fact, according to Henrik, by five Magnus had climbed Galdhøpiggen, the tallest mountain in northern Europe. Magnus pressed on for most of the way on his own, until his father finally picked up his exhausted child and carried him the rest of the way.

But it was chess that quickly became Magnus's principal obsession. His memory and tactical supremacy verged on the occult. He could gleefully play blindfolded against ten opponents in ten separate simultaneous games and almost casually hold the progress of 320 pieces and the infinite possibilities regarding where they might move in his mind as he slaughtered all chal-lengers. When Bob Simon witnessed such an exhibition in 2012 for a *60 Minutes* profile, he breathlessly described the demon-stration as "the most amazing thing I've ever seen. . . . It seems to transcend chess. I can't fathom what you've done. It's just . . . supernatural."

But while Magnus's talents might have been supernatural, his motivations were as human as they come: namely, revenge. School for Magnus was a minefield of navigating bullies and surviving their torments. Chess offered both an escape and a way to exact retribution. He took out his helplessness and humiliation on his opponents. He sadistically savored their agony, enjoyed inflict-ing suffering on anyone who dared oppose his will. And he didn't keep this lurid fact to himself either.

"But you enjoy it when you see your opponent squirm?" Bob Simon asked Magnus.

"Yes," Magnus acknowledged soberly, "I *do*. I enjoy it when I see my opponent really suffering."

The title of that *60 Minutes* profile was "The Mozart of Chess." *60 Minutes* didn't come up with that. That was what *Washington Post* chess writer Lubomir Kavalek called Magnus after the way he dominated a game in Holland in 2004. "He was 13 at that time," Kavalek wrote in his final column for the paper in 2010, "and, ac-cording to my good friend, the late *Washington Post* music critic Joseph McLellan, he was too old to be compared to the great music composer. But it was too late. The name stuck." However, it was a blitz tournament—where players compete with drastically less time on the clock than in conventional chess matches—in Reyk-javík later that same year that served as Magnus's true coming-out party. It put the chess world on notice that a terror on the board was emerging.

First, Magnus—then ranked seven hundredth in the world—beat the legendary Anatoly Karpov, who had succeeded Bobby Fischer as the game's dominant player, reigning as world champion from 1975 to 1985. Then Magnus faced off against Kasparov, who had defeated Karpov to become world champion and was still the top-ranked player in the world. Kasparov was twenty-eight years older than Carlsen and had never played against anyone so young in a formal tournament.

Kasparov kept Carlsen waiting alone at the table for thirty minutes beyond the assigned starting time. The innocent-looking boy, armed only with a massive Pepsi bottle filled with orange juice and swimming in a black hoodie, calmly set up his pieces and adjusted them on their squares while he waited for his adversary to arrive. Carlsen looked around and, not seeing his opponent in the room, opened a coffee-table book to no particular page and leafed through until he found a landscape that captivated his interest. Other players slapped their clocks to begin the afternoon's games while Carlsen leisurely wandered around the room with his hands in his pockets, observing the openings. His father sat nervously in the audience, with Magnus's mother and two sisters, staring at his son, who meandered over to the refreshments table to pour himself a glass of Coke.

Magnus had been taken out from school for that entire year by his parents. Already known in Norway as a celebrity prodigy, he had been playing before large crowds in shopping malls and putting on displays of his shocking chess virtuosity in dazzling simultaneous exhibitions in which he played against numerous opponents. Carlsen was beginning to come out of his shell and enjoy the attention of crowds marveling at his abilities on the board.

When Kasparov finally arrived, dressed in a dark three-piece suit, he took his seat, swung his jacket behind his chair, and began fussing with the black side's pieces and dusting off squares on the board with his fingertips. Magnus reached over, pushed his pawn forward, and struck his clock. Kasparov dropped his head into his hands in concentration. Carlsen played with his lips while he studied Kasparov's face with benign curiosity. As the game progressed, Kasparov became increasingly fidgety, running through a marvelous display of animated signature frazzled expressions—shaking his head, incessantly brushing back his hair, rubbing his face, leaning back in his chair and forcing his eyes wide open like a horse's in fire—until finally he assumed the posture of Rodin's *Thinker* while his clock ticked down and he pondered his next move.

At that point, Carlsen noticed something and seemed to lose interest in the drama of the most important game of his life. This was the most transcendently beautiful moment of Carlsen's career up to that point. He had seen the game's conclusion in his mind already, even before his masterful, infinitely more experienced opponent. Carlsen nonchalantly turned in his chair and looked across the room at some other tables, and for one of the only times in the game, Kasparov, seething, glared across the board for an instant at Carlsen's half-drunk glass of Coke. Carlsen spun around further in his chair to look at other games, absentmindedly rose to his feet, jammed his hands in his pockets, and walked out of the spotlight into the shadows to matter-of-factly stroll around the other boards.

Kasparov refused to look away from his pieces, yet when he

made his move he struck his clock with some frustrated emphasis. Carlsen returned to his seat immediately and instantly moved his pawn in response. There was an almost playfully casual menace in his eyes as he watched Kasparov's face betray hope circling the drain.

Finally Kasparov offered his hand for a draw, exploded out of his chair like an ejecting F-16 pilot, and yanked his coat on as he stormed off. Kasparov gave one last fleeting glance at the battlefield over the board and noticed Magnus turning back to look at him. Magnus tried to keep a straight face and finally threw up his hands, annoyed that he'd given up a winning position. His family rewarded him for his draw with Kasparov with a visit to McDonald's and some ice cream.

Unlike the rest of the chess world, Carlsen was disappointed with his performance. To him, a draw against a world champion felt like a mild failure. With a smirk, he confessed to Bob Simon of *60 Minutes*, "When I actually got the winning position I had little time. I was nervous and I couldn't finish him off. . . . I was playing Kasparov. I was intimidated."

Only a month later, Carlsen achieved the rating of grandmaster. At thirteen years, four months, and twenty-seven days, he was the second youngest player ever to receive the distinction. The youngest had achieved it in 2002, at twelve years and seven months, a record which still stands to this day.

His name? Sergey Karjakin.

For the first time in twenty-one years, since he began playing chess at five, Karjakin could clearly see the dream that had uprooted his entire family and caused them to abandon the country of his birth.

At five and a half years old, Karjakin encountered chess for the first time on television, and his father brought out a chessboard so the two could play together. The first chess school where Karjakin would train, soon after, was located only a hundred meters from where he was born. One of the greatest prodigies in the history of chess was on his way. But, by virtue of nothing more than the accident of where he was born, Simferopol, a city of three hundred thousand on the Crimean Peninsula, Karjakin did not have the opportunity to spend his formative years engaged in serious study and training with top professionals, as Carlsen did. As a teen, Karjakin enjoyed none of Carlsen's upper-middle-class comforts. His father was unable to support his family on a cook's wages, and Karjakin and his parents were forced to live in a cramped three-room apartment with his grandparents, supplementing their income by selling whatever they could on the street.

Karjakin's talents on the board were so conspicuous that as a five-year-old he was featured on Ukrainian television. Only seven years after he first moved a chess piece, his brilliance and obsession with following that chess piece wherever it might take him allowed him to become, at twelve, the youngest grandmaster in history. Shortly after he began competing, Karjakin's conspicuous talents were noticed by a businessman named Alexander Momot, who invited Sergey to study at his school in the Donetsk region of eastern Ukraine. The entire Karjakin family left behind their lives in Simferopol to support Karjakin's dream. "We sacrificed everything so he could be a world champion," Alexander Karjakin, Sergey's father, confessed to filmmaker Alexander Turpin in the documentary *Sergey*. And, in turn, his son dutifully sacrificed his own childhood to devote his tireless energies to the game of chess.

Soon after, Sergey boasted in his soft, childish voice on local talk shows that he expected to win the world championship at sixteen. Fate sabotaged Karjakin's plans when the director of his chess school died and the school promptly closed down. Karjakin and his family were forced to move back to Simferopol, where the prodigy received no support for his training and coaching. "From twelve years old until nineteen years old," Karjakin remembered, "when I moved to Moscow, I didn't have any support from the government, from sponsors, just nothing. It was very difficult. We had to invite some coaches to pay them all their expenses, and at that time I didn't earn that much. Magnus had very good support from sponsors from the time he was twelve or something like that, and at that time, he was clearly not as good as me. He had much easier opportunities than me."

In April 2005, Karjakin broke into the world's top one hundred rated players.

But, by 2009, the lack of financial support led his entire family to leave their jobs and uproot themselves so that he could accept the Russian Chess Federation's offer to finance him and his training costs along with providing housing. In return, Karjakin renounced his Ukrainian citizenship for a Russian passport and moved with his family to Moscow. Once in Russia, Karjakin's progress was nurtured by Yury Dokhoian, the longtime coach of Garry Kasparov. A year before his move to Moscow, Karjakin had risen to the world's thirteenth-best player, yet by his nineteenth birthday he had sunk fourteen spots to twenty-seventh. Finally surrounded by the best coaching of his life, Karjakin again set his sights on his childhood dream of becoming world champion.

But Karjakin remained a man with a grievance, as if through

circumstance he had been exiled from his birthright in the game, explaining in a recent televised interview from Moscow's chess museum, "Maybe if I had moved to Russia earlier, it would have been even easier for me to develop faster than I did." His father, Alexander Karjakin, explained, "We sacrificed everything so that he could become a world champion. . . . I think I did the right thing. It's too late to do anything about it." After Russia had thoroughly dominated the second half of the twentieth century with world champions, Karjakin was fighting to become the first Russian world champion since Vladimir Kramnik held the title in 2007.

Soon after his move to Moscow, Karjakin successfully competed against his former teammates on behalf of Russia at the Chess Olympiad. Many of his old coaches and friends were afraid to even speak with him given his public statements on Crimea. After Russia's highly controversial annexation in 2014, which led to sanctions from the United States, Karjakin wore T-shirts with Vladimir Putin's likeness. In Russian, Karjakin sarcastically tweeted of his hometown: "If I don't return home, then my home returns to me," concluding with a smiley face and Russian flag emoji.

Putin's investment seemed to have paid off.

Karjakin's very qualification for the championship match had been a surprise for most chess experts. He won the Candidates Tournament held in Moscow the previous March (a competition akin to something like eight lanes' worth of qualifiers squaring off at the Olympic hundred-meter dash semifinal, except run on quaaludes to produce chronically catatonic, glacial drama) after having entered as the second lowest ranking player, at thirteenth in the world. He was now ranked eighth and had defeated former world champion Viswanathan Anand (whom Carlsen won the championship from in 2013) for the first time in his career. In the final round, he faced American Fabiano Caruana, the third highest ranked player in the tournament. Caruana had grown up in Park Slope, Brooklyn, and, with victory, offered the New York media a homegrown story peg to hang stories on at the world championship.

Caruana had been the highest rated player to compete for the chance to challenge Carlsen at the Candidates Tournament. He lived up to expectations and rolled into the final round, potentially only needing a draw to win the tournament. In the finals, Caruana wasted little time making it abundantly clear on the board he intended to play for the win with his Classical Sicilian. Even playing with black pieces, Caruana's early aggression looked like it could be rewarded, only for Karjakin to find a fatal flaw in his defenses. On the forty-second move, Caruana pounced for a win. Karjakin responded with sacrificing his rook to not just defend his position but ingeniously create a winning attack. Once he had the advantage, Karjakin never let go until Caruana was forced to resign on the forty-fourth move. New York and the United States were denied a hometown kid fighting for the chance to become the first American-born chess player to be world champion since Bobby Fischer.

So instead, prior to the start of the match, the media focused on Karjakin's connection to Russia. When the *New York Post* asked him about it, he said, "Putin wished me good luck and asked how my training is going. The Russian government gives a lot of things for me to feel comfortable." Putin was also rumored to be sending his press security, Dmitry Peskov, to lend support to Karjakin.

One Russian with ties to Putin who wouldn't be there was

FIDE president Kirsan Ilyumzhinov. As far as totally surreal, out-landish, larger than life characters to interview from the chess world (or anywhere else, for that matter), nobody on paper looked more fun to interview than Ilyumzhinov. His deranged ramblings gave L. Ron Hubbard and anything Xenu creation myth–oriented reserved for Scientologists at Operating Thetan Level 8 a run for their money. From the opening paragraph of nearly anything written about him, Ilyumzhinov was more nightmarishly car-toonish than *anything* inflicted on the public from the demented imagination of Sacha Baron Cohen, the key difference being that Ilyumzhinov was real and wielding real power over the small coun-try he ruled. His unhinged psychosis had made a calamity of the lives of hundreds of thousands of people.

Ilyumzhinov got involved in chess after being inspired by Bobby Fischer's victory against Boris Spassky, and took over con-trol of FIDE in 1995. Two years later, in 1997, he claimed to have been abducted by aliens and maintained that extraterrestrials were responsible for the invention of chess two thousand years ago. He also had enjoyed relationships with Saddam Hussein and Syria's Bashar al-Assad, and played chess with Libyan leader Mu'ammar Gaddafi in a tent shortly before his death. Ilyumzhinov had been sanctioned by the US the previous year for purported deals with the Assad regime and banned from entering the country. Ilyumzhi-nov had recently stated to the BBC that the Syrian president, whose exploits included overseeing torture, murder of political op-ponents, summarily executing between five thousand and thirteen thousand citizens in mass hangings, along with recent chemical attacks against his own people, including those that killed dozens of children, should be nominated for a Nobel Peace Prize.

Ilyumzhinov was himself a head of state—the president of the Russian republic of Kalmykia from 1993 to 2010. He supposedly used telepathic powers to stay connected with his brutally impoverished people. While Kalmykia's three hundred thousand citizens lived in some of the most wretchedly poor conditions on earth—often devoid of electricity and clean drinking water—Ilyumzhinov looted the coffers of Kalmykia and dropped an obscene personal fortune to build something called Chess City. It was a cross between a chess Walt Disney World and a chess Vatican, replete with a chess-centric neighborhood boasting a four-story domed City Chess Hall and surrounding village, and a chess museum, just for starters, to accommodate hosting duties for Chess Olympiads and two World Chess Championships (first the women's in 2004 and then the men's in 2006).

Ilyumzhinov secured Chess City with armed guards and menacing barbed-wire fences and boasted about plans to build a skiing center, water sports complex, an opera house, a conservatory, more museums, an art gallery, and business centers. Frequently Ilyumzhinov handed out diamond tiaras to tournament winners. When a journalist investigated what he was doing, the journalist was kidnapped and murdered by two men, one of whom had worked as a former presidential bodyguard.

Ilyumzhinov also attempted to make Chess City the home of Bobby Fischer, tracking him down in Budapest to offer $100,000 to make amends for pirated editions of his books sold on the black market in the Soviet Union. As far gone as Fischer was at that point, he wouldn't go along with Ilyumzhinov's plans.

Even without Ilyumzhinov there, it was hard not to see the parallels between the way Russia inserted itself in the US election and the extent to which it was involved in the championship. It was rumored that Carlsen himself had called Microsoft for assistance with growing fears of Russian hackers targeting the high-powered chess computers he used for analysis and strategy in the lead-up to the championship match.

Microsoft first began sponsoring Magnus in 2004, and the way in which that represented a shift in the game's attitude toward technology was one of the most significant storylines of the championship.

It was Alan Turing, the man who famously cracked the Nazi Enigma code, who invented the first chess computer program, in 1952. He created a chess algorithm on pieces of paper. But it would take nearly half a century for computers to catch up to human players. After beating an IBM chess computer in 1989, Garry Kasparov had taunted IBM's designers with some useful advice, "Teach it to resign earlier."

By 1996, Kasparov was just as confident of his ability to compete against IBM's Deep Blue. When organizers proposed a 60/40 split of the $500,000 purse shared between the winner and loser, Kasparov, according to *Time*, preferred a zero-sum game. On February 10, 1996, Kasparov sat down to play his first of a six-game match against Deep Blue in the Pennsylvania Convention Center in Philadelphia. The computer made the first move with white pieces, and after Kasparov responded, Deep Blue began its frightening hundred-million-different-chess-positions-per-second evaluation. Despite what he was up against, Kasparov was favored to win the match by the oddsmakers. But after Deep Blue's thirty-seventh move, Kasparov resigned. A chess-playing computer had defeated a reigning world champion for the first time in history, and according to his coach, Kasparov was "shattered." But he rebounded the next day, and after a marathon seventy-three-move game, up on material, Deep Blue's operator resigned. The next two games ended in draws. In the fifth game, playing black no less, Kasparov took control. On the twenty-third move, Kasparov offered Deep Blue a draw, which was declined. This proved unwise. Kasparov took the game twenty-four moves later, the only game in the match won by black. On February 17, Kasparov won the sixth game and the match.

The rematch in New York, on May 3 of the following year, was the highest-profile match chess had had since Fischer-Spassky, twenty-five years earlier. It was Man vs. Machine, with *Newsweek* running a cover story about it called "The Brain's Last Stand." At the time, the event was the largest internet event in history.

IBM invested $20 million in their supercomputer and rented several floors of the Equitable Center in Midtown Manhattan to store their machine. Kasparov has frequently remarked in the media that IBM hired more security to guard Deep Blue than the Pentagon employed to guard any of their top computers. Deep Blue defeated Kasparov in the final game of their six-game match, in fewer than twenty moves. IBM stock rose 15 percent on the day they defeated Kasparov, and within a week, their stock value would rise an estimated $11.4 billion in worth. They refused to offer Kasparov a rematch.

Despite mutual agreement on all the terms before the match, Kasparov accused the IBM team of dirty tricks. He became the first reigning world champion ever to lose a game to a chess-playing computer, garnering the most attention of his career by losing to a machine. He described it as both his "blessing and curse" to be the "John Henry of chess." The loss was so painful that for the next twenty years he would "avoid and deflect" any discussion about his match against Deep Blue.

Back then, Kasparov was held up to be defending not just chess against artificial intelligence but all of humanity. According to Erik Brynjolfsson, MIT professor and author of *Race Against the Machine*, "The new Machine Age can be dated to a day when Garry Kasparov, the world chess champion, played Deep Blue, a supercomputer." Despite Trump's campaigning about bad trade deals, vilifying China and Mexico, offshoring, and undocumented immigrants being responsible for taking American jobs, the biggest culprit, according to many economists, has been automation. Lawrence Katz, an economics professor at Harvard who studies labor and technological change, told the *New York Times* in late 2016, "Over the long haul, clearly automation's been much more important—it's not even close." Automation, like all technological advance, offers no clear way to halt its progress. Trump's pick for labor secretary, Andrew F. Puzder, gave an interview with *Business Insider* lauding the advantages of robot employees over humans, declaring, "They're always polite, they always upsell, they never take a vacation, they never show up late, there's never a slip-and-fall, or an age, sex, or race discrimination case." According to a Gallup poll conducted in late 2017, nearly five in six Americans currently use a product or service that features artificial intelligence. But while the vast majority of Americans anticipate artificial intelligence will contribute to job losses within the next ten years, interestingly only a minority believe *their* jobs are at risk. And just as there's no going back on an automated economy, computers are now an integral part of chess.

In 1977, five years after beating Boris Spassky to become world champion and a Cold War symbolic conqueror of the Soviets for the United States, Bobby Fischer was on the lam descending into paranoid psychosis in Pasadena, California. Fischer had joined a cult prophesying the looming apocalypse. He'd removed fillings from his teeth to avoid detection by radioactive signals from the Russians and Israeli Mossad agents. He lived in a rattrap apartment covered in tinfoil. Despite Fischer's mental deterioration and not having competed in a game of chess in half a decade, he sent handwritten letters to computer scientist Hans Berliner expressing his interest in "the computer chess scene." Fischer inquired if Berliner could assist him in being involved. Soon after, Fischer traveled in disguise to Cambridge, Massachusetts, to play against the highest powered computer program developed by an MIT engineer, and in all three games, Fischer mated the machine. Fischer disappeared soon after.

However, the same year Fischer thrashed AI's most powerful representative on the chessboard, a computer chess pioneer named Monty Newborn offered this ominous prophesy: "Chess masters used to come to computer chess tournaments to laugh. Now they come to watch. Soon they will come to learn."

The reason the internet melted down in 1997 as Deep Blue marched its armies against Kasparov in defense of humanity was, according to MIT economics professor Erik Brynjolfsson, there was recognition that the new Machine Age had begun. Kasparov famously compared competing against Deep Blue to playing against "God." The first time Kasparov lost to Deep Blue in

1996, despondent, he went back to his hotel room, disrobed to his underwear, and despairingly stared at the ceiling.

Today, any child spectator watching Carlsen and Karjakin with a chess app on their phone could annihilate not just the future world champion with ease, but any chess player ever born. There's infinitely more technology on their phone than what sent human beings to the moon. For decades, AI has functioned something like Thor's hammer looking for nails. And now no chess grandmaster can compete without a computer engine's guidance in molding their game. With massive corporate backing and top engineer teams at the helm, AI has laid waste to human intelligence in checkers, Jeopardy, backgammon, Chinese chess, poker, Scrabble, Go, Othello, shogi, and Connect Four. Board games are a done deal. IBM's Deep Blue was capable of eleven billion operations per second and was the 259th-fastest supercomputer in the world in 1997. The equivalent hardware today is *sixty thousand* times faster.

Back in 1968, Stanley Kubrick's *2001: A Space Odyssey* tapped into humanity's anxiety about AI and even subtly informed viewers with the first clue of the HAL 9000's eventual descent into madness while the machine is playing chess with Dr. Frank Poole: "I'm sorry Frank," HAL calmly remarks, "I think you missed it: Queen to Bishop three, Bishop takes Queen, Knight takes Bishop, mate." The move in question is, in fact, an illegal move. The correct move is Queen to Bishop six. Kubrick, a chess fanatic, the most obsessively detail-oriented director in film history, likely didn't insert this error by accident. Arthur C. Clarke, *2001*'s author, was once asked to write a science-fiction story that could fit on the back of a postcard. His 1977 story "Quarantine," about an alien civilization destroying Earth after they discovered chess on it and became obsessed with it ("We had no choice: five earlier units became totally infected, when they made contact."), was published in *Isaac Asimov's Science Fiction Magazine*.

In 2007, computers worked through every available move in the game of checkers and revealed the ideal game to "solve" checkers. In 2011, IBM's Watson steamrolled Ken Jennings on *Jeopardy!* Maybe one day computers will solve chess and create a game unsolvable for themselves. The broader implications of Deep Blue's victory as a harbinger of technology *off* the board are eerie to contemplate in our increasingly automated world. Automation has taken more American jobs than global trade. The industrial revolution took place over seventy years. The adjustment to this change has created a whiplash effect. According to Brynjolfsson, author of *Race Against the Machine*, "Computers get better faster than anything else *ever*. A child's PlayStation today is more powerful than a military supercomputer from 1996." After only a decade since its invention, there are billions of smartphones scattered across the world and 1.5 million Android phones activated daily. If Bill Gates and Mark Zuckerberg *had* shown up as advertised at the World Chess Championship, they, along with the other six wealthiest people on earth, controlled the same amount of wealth as the bottom half of the planet's population.

Twenty years after Deep Blue trounced humanity's best hope on the chessboard, the event seems to resonate even more deeply now, as though Kubrick's *2001* monolith were tripping a silent cosmic burglar alarm. Before Kasparov's fall to Deep Blue, Dutch chess grandmaster Jan-Hein Donner was asked how he'd prepare for a match against a machine and famously replied, "I would bring a hammer."

While computers have pushed and elevated accuracy in chess to levels surpassing anything humans could achieve on their own, no computer has played a game of the kind of arresting beauty, the harmony and poetry, that characterizes the matches chess aficionados marvel at. Their games are bloodless. "Computers are useless," Picasso once remarked. "They can only give you answers." The real danger starts when (and not *if*) they started asking questions. With computers, today's games are more or less Auto-Tuned to unravel human creativity. The greatest artists in chess were simultaneously sublime composers and masterful terrorists smuggling in explosives to detonate in battle against their opponents. Blood, sweat, and tears are not a binary operation. The board may be black-and-white, and computations a series of zeroes and ones, but the human dimension resides in the gray matter of a place the machine can never inhabit.

Whatever domination AI has wrought against humans in intellectual endeavors, where are the great symphonies, novels, or paintings it has created? For over fifteen hundred years, chess has mysteriously offered its unique backstage pass to both consciousness and the human condition. Maybe this was why, despite humanity's inferiority and limitations in ability relative to machines, the world still looked to its finest living chess players for a fresh glimpse of the mysteries and art in the game of chess, hoping to uncover an oasis that still resides exclusively in the human imagination.

# 3

# TROMPOWSKY

The championship was the first big event to take place in the Fulton Market Building since Hurricane Sandy had devastated Lower Manhattan's South Street Seaport neighborhood four years earlier. The area had been in bad shape for a couple years after the storm, with shops closed, some buildings boarded up or even abandoned, and local papers referring to the area as a "ghost town." The National Trust for Historic Preservation had named it one of the most endangered historic places in the country. But thanks to $10 million in FEMA money, businesses were starting to reopen and the place was coming back. Christmas carol Muzak drifted through the air as I walked toward the building on that cold, windy morning of November 11—the first day of the championship.

It was my second time there in two days. I'd come down the

morning before to cover the opening press conference. I'd wondered what a world championship press conference looked like
with chess. Boxing and chess swapped metaphors from each other's
racket endlessly. When Bobby Fischer played Boris Spassky in Iceland for the world title in 1972, he set his sights on Muhammad
Ali as someone whose pay his own should measure up to. When
Norman Mailer showed up in Zaire (now the Democratic Republic
of the Congo) for George Foreman and Ali's press conference in
1974, he recorded these words for his book *The Fight*:

> *"Oh, I'm the greatest fighter who ever lived. I'm a wonder. The
> fifth wonder of the world. I'm even faster than Muhammad Ali.
> And I'm going to knock him out in three . . . two . . . one."*
>
> *"Foreman's nothing but a hard-push puncher. He can't hit!
> He's never knocked a man out . . . he just got slow punches, take
> a year to get there."*
>
> *"He makes me think of a parrot who keeps saying, 'You're
> stupid, you're stupid.' Not to offend Muhammad Ali, but he's like
> that parrot. What he says, he's said before."*
>
> *"I say to you in the press, you are impressed with Foreman
> because he looks like a big Black man and he hits a bag so
> hard. . . . But I let you in on a secret. Colored folks scare more
> white folks than they scare colored folks. I am not afraid of Fore-
> man, and that you will discover."*

That fight, the famous "Rumble in the Jungle," was covered by
the likes of Mailer, George Plimpton, and Hunter S. Thompson.
Here in the small, packed conference room were a couple of reporters from major outlets like the BBC and the *New York Times*.

But mostly it was writers and bloggers from arcane chess periodicals and websites. And it was quickly apparent there would be none of that brazen shit-talk from Magnus and Sergey. Neither had Fischer's knack for being especially quotable, especially for anyone outside the chess world.

"Who do you consider the best chess player in the world?" one reporter asked.

The assembled journalists laughed. Magnus smiled.

"I think that's going to be decided in the next couple of weeks, no?" he said. "But . . . um . . . yes . . . um . . . right now, if I may be so bold, I would say myself . . . yeah."

The same question was asked of Sergey.

"Yeah, I can basically agree with Magnus that at the moment he's world champion. But in a few weeks we will know who will win the match."

Sergey was asked how he was liking New York City. It was his first time there.

"I like the place very much," he said. "Basically I feel very comfortable. Yeah, it's . . . yeah, I'm fine."

Reporter: "What do you think your opponent's best quality is, and how do you prepare to defeat it?"

Magnus: "I think Sergey is very well prepared. He has studied the game very well. Very knowledgeable. And most of all he's extremely resilient. In defense, he's very, very good at finding resources even in difficult positions. He can defend. And I guess for me it's a matter of when I get the chance I'll try to punch him until he finally knocks over."

Sergey: "Magnus has a lot of advantages. He's been in many tournaments. He's world champion. But I don't want to comment on the chess part much. Of course I made some preparation. But I want to keep some secrets."

The only remotely entertaining exchange took place when a reporter asked Magnus about a report that he had enlisted Microsoft's help in thwarting Russian hacking of his computer preparation. Both Magnus and Sergey laughed, and Magnus said, "Well, I mean, I think it has to be said that the fear of hacking and everything, that was not the words of me or anyone from my team. We have, in general, systems to make work easier for me and my team. But we are not fearing attacks from Sergey and his team."

Again, they both smiled. And when Sergey was asked if he was taking any precautions against hacking, he said, "Yes, but not as much as Magnus. I just downloaded some antivirus."

At some point the BBC reporter asked how embarrassing it was that Ilyumzhinov wasn't able to be there.

At the end of the long dais were FIDE vice president Israel Gelfer and Agon Limited CEO Ilya Merenzon. They leaned away from their microphones and whispered to each other for about a minute, trying to figure out what to say.

"We all know that there is some case between FIDE president Kirsan Ilyumzhinov and the United States authorities," Gelfer finally said. "But I don't think we should discuss it here. This is a press conference dedicated to the match and not to political questions. And I don't think we should comment on this. If you like to have some political questions, that's not the time for this. We don't have to comment on this, I think."

After ten minutes the moderator turned the line of questioning toward the two main sponsors: the Moscow-based asset-management firm EG Capital Advisors and the Russian fertilizer company PhosAgro. It might have been hosted in New York, but this championship was as American as an apple pie baked in the Kremlin's kitchen and flown into Teterboro, New Jersey, by private jet.

"What's important about chess is that this game is in Russian DNA," said a PhosAgro spokesperson when asked by the moderator why the company was sponsoring the event. "Because when you're born, you start to play chess with your grandfather or father. Then you go to school, kindergarten or whatever, and you continue. I would bet ninety-nine percent of Russian citizen [*sic*] they play chess. And for us as a Russian business it was a fantastic and historical opportunity."

Then Merenzon talked for a bit about how the championship was "a coming-out party for chess" and how it would usher in a "renaissance" for the game and how "more people play chess than golf and tennis . . . *combined*!" With his shaved head and thick neck, he looked more as though he were from the boxing world I was used to covering. And he was the only person to deliver the kind of bitchy banter I'd shown up for. When I was introduced to him after the thirty-minute press conference ended, he looked at my attire (khaki pants and leather jacket) with mild disgust, scoffed, and said, "You should go home and change into a suit."

On the morning of the match, despite fairly steep prices and Trump's election dominating all the news, a considerable crowd formed at the entrance long before the event. A misfit horde of fifty photographers and journalists were waiting around for credentials alongside the crowd. Eventually we were marched through a security detail waving metal-detector wands. We stepped onto a long escalator that belonged in a cartoon connecting the recently departed with heaven.

On the way up, a middle-aged stranger saw my press credentials and jovially asked my chess rating.

"Over two thousand?" he speculated generously.

Before I could answer, he laughingly admitted he'd been so hooked on chess during high school and all the tournaments he was playing that he had to find something less stressful.

"I had to give it up. I just had to. Instead of chess I devoted myself to becoming a cardiologist. But it never gets out of your blood. I only let myself play half a dozen games a day online. That's my limit."

I noticed the VIP bracelet around his wrist.

"You paid twelve hundred dollars to watch today's game?" I asked him.

"On top of the flight from Colorado and the hotel," he said.

I wasn't sure if this was a demonstration of something profane or sacred. Eighteen months earlier, I'd covered the Floyd Mayweather–Manny Pacquiao fight in Las Vegas. Some seats had sold for $375,000, which had led to a record-breaking total gate of $75 million. An additional four and a half million people had paid $100 each to watch on pay-per-view. The two participants on display, who hardly engaged in combat over the course of twelve rounds, earned $400 million for thirty-six minutes of work. So in some sense dropping more than a grand to watch an hours-long chess game was a bargain. Still, I was taken aback.

"I couldn't miss this," the cardiologist said. "Chess at *this* level? These guys can lose as much weight during a chess game as a boxer during a fight. Look what happened with Karpov and Kasparov."

"What happened?" I asked.

The cardiologist's eyes lit up.

"When they played at the 1984 world championship," he said, "the winner was decided by the first player to six victories. Kasparov was soon down zero to four. Then he lost another.

"He was only twenty-one. Karpov was in his mid-thirties. So Kasparov decided to break Karpov's health. Over the next forty-one games, Kasparov had one victory and dealt Karpov forty draws. Kasparov's victory, in Game thirty-two, was his first ever against the world champion.

"During that loss and all those grueling draws, Karpov had lost twenty-two pounds. He was suffering from exhaustion. The longest world title match ever, before this one, was José Raúl Capablanca playing thirty-four games in 1927.

"Game forty-seven, Kasparov scores a win after fifteen draws in a row. It's five–two. Karpov's lead is slipping. Worse, he's fading horribly. Game forty-eight, Kasparov wins another.

"The president of FIDE flies over to Moscow and declares the match over out of concern for the players' health. Both players protest, wanting the match to continue. They're overruled. It's the only world championship in history that ended without a winner.

"I can't even begin to imagine the kind of strain and pressure Magnus and Sergey are walking into when they sit down at the board. Every game of this thing is like watching Gary Cooper in *High Noon*. The tension is excruciating."

The escalator finally deposited us on the upper level of the building. All throughout the space, chessboards and polished pieces were set up. Kids raced to find empty chairs. I watched the cardiologist bask in the joy of seeing dozens of clocks unsheathed from bags, like Excalibur ripped from the stone, and armies of pieces sorted by rank and immaculately positioned on their designated squares.

In the post-match conference room, dozens of TV cameras were being set up. A glassed-in commentators' booth was off to the side. There, a team that included Judit Polgár, the greatest female player in history, would be calling the play-by-play. Really, though, they would be making small talk *between* the play-by-play, what with the games routinely running longer than five or six hours and *huge* spans of time between moves.

There was no escape from the looping EG Capital and Phos-Agro commercials—incessant groaning about sound financial planning and fertilizer came from large flat-screens scattered all over. They weren't the only sponsors. There was also Isklar, a Norwegian bottled water that sponsored Magnus. I saw a journalist twist off a cap and take a gulp and I asked him how it tasted. In a conspicuous Scandinavian accent he grinned and lifted his chin like Colonel Kilgore from *Apocalypse Now*: "It tastes like . . . *victory*." One of the organizers proudly led me to the display of another sponsor, S. T. Dupont, a Paris-based maker of pens, lighters, cigar humidors, cigar cutters, cuff links, money clips, tie clips, and sundry leather goods like belts, bags, wallets, business-card holders, and key rings. In an exclusive VIP lounge, their ornate pens and lighters were on display behind glass, including the hand-sculpted, gold tone–lacquered Phoenix Renaissance Limited Edition, adorned with two precious citrine stones, its mythical namesake having "offered its wings to the master goldsmiths to adorn their hallmark"—all of it looking like a handsome and fetching Third Reich Love-Letter-Writing-and-Postcoital-Smoke Dream Set marketed to people still swooning over Hitler and Eva Braun's torrid romance. And what a steal at just under $12,000! The VIP lounge also had an open bar where the featured drink was something called Beluga vodka ("noble Russian vodka," according to the bottle, Siberian distilled!).

Then there was the room where the two players would face off. It was minimally furnished. Just a table and two chairs—the high-backed leather office kind you get at Staples. In front of each chair was a pad of paper and an S. T. Dupont pen. There was a small alcove to the side with a couch and bottled water and snacks. Here the players could get up and walk around and hang out while their opponents contemplated their next move.

One wall of the room was made of glass, so that spectators could observe. The playing space was like a diorama in a museum or a police interrogation room with a one-way mirror. Or maybe the best analogy of all is that it recalled a staging area for a hanging or an electrocution. Because by the end of this match one of these two men's dreams would be dead—whether Magnus's hopes of being acknowledged outright as the greatest player who'd ever lived or Sergey's fantasy of proving after all these years that he was a champion. The confined space was suffocating, a symbolic execution chamber. Except the glass here wasn't tinted. And unlike with real executions, where the members of the firing squad are spared a dirty conscience via the presence of a lone bullet that could be in *any* gun, or the hangman's identity is concealed with a mask, here the one marked for death could witness the voyeuristic pleasure of both audience and assassin. The face of your sadistic killer was directly in front of you savoring every moment, massacring all your defenses, gradually running a straight-edge razor over your king's jugular. And if you'd given your entire life to defending a three-and-a-half-inch game piece's existence on the board, what would happen to your identity when you proved inept as its imperial guard?

While that small room made me think of an execution chamber, looking out over the hall of spectators, at the people scattered around playing speed chess at tables or even on the floor, having brought their own boards and pieces from home, I felt eerily like Gulliver stranded on the flying island of Laputa.

Laputa was a kingdom whose occupants were feverishly devoted to pursuits like music, mathematics, technology, and astronomy, yet were unable to find much practical application for their obsessions. Jonathan Swift paints the inhabitants of the floating island as being so lost in their own worlds that a vast segment of society is enslaved solely to whip them with "bladders" and bring them, however briefly, back to reality. The assembly of geniuses in Laputa's castle are so focused on their intellectual pursuits that their clothes don't fit, that their homes are poorly built, and Gulliver soon discovers what ruin is wrought in a society so tyrannically invested in such confined and narrow obsessions.

The most powerful nation in human history was about to hand the nuclear codes to an irascible, pompous reality-TV star, and I had the distinct impression that no one present could possibly care less. It was right back to that eerie game-room-in-*Titanic* feeling.

A member of the Fulton Market Building's staff walked across the room with two cans of Febreze—Meadows & Rain scent—in either fist, fumigating the floor.

"Did a kid have an accident?" I asked.

"No," he said. "With this crowd it's more of a general hygiene issue."

I'm not sure what I was expecting in terms of a championship-chess crowd, but it was a hybrid of several distinctive camps I'd never seen assembled in the same place before. None of them mixed. When the kids in the crowd saw the chessboards laid out and raced over to play, they made the venue feel like a carnival petting zoo. Observing those games with studious attention, the group of nearsighted, disheveled, middle-aged men in wrinkled clothes presumably being attended to by the cans of Febreze were straight out of central casting from an Atlantic City, hung-out-to-dry, post-casino, 2 a.m. Greyhound bus station. Everywhere else I looked, surly Steven Seagal–type Russian men in fine suits mingled and milled around the facility with Bond-girl foreign women attired in cocktail dresses.

Then Magnus Carlsen arrived with a retinue of aides from a private stairwell and simultaneously lit the fuse of all the camps in attendance. Carlsen's father broke off from the team to answer some questions for reporters while photographers encircled his son and a constellation of flashes erupted. As the camera flashes popped, Magnus, dressed in a crisp suit emblazoned with patches bearing the logos of his corporate sponsors, looked relaxed and buoyantly contemptuous of his surroundings. He carried himself with the demeanor of an established genius still very much on the rise with the best yet to come. All at once the Fulton Market spectators froze and fell silent as they observed the young champion.

His arrogance wasn't off-putting: in having delivered on his promise as a child prodigy to become who he was, he reminded those in the room just how many prodigies fail to arrive on the world stage with anything resembling the allure that first captured the public's imagination. Magnus's demeanor seemed to suggest that being the world's best was just the beginning of his ambition—that he was gunning for being the best ever.

I turned to see how Carlsen's father, Henrik, was holding up under the pressure. The fathers of chess prodigies often play the unsettling role of first sacrificial victim that their children must vanquish, forever staining the board. Others, like Fischer, found the chessboard in no small part because they grew up fatherless. Kasparov lost his father to leukemia at the age of seven. One wondered which baptism, that of patricidal blood or that of isolation, might inflict more damage at such a tender age. "The loss of my childhood was the price of becoming the youngest world champion in history," Kasparov once stated. "When you have to fight every day from a young age, your soul could become contaminated. . . . I became a soldier too early."

Henrik looked over at his son and waved off any further questions. Together they briskly strolled into the VIP section.

Sergey and his team followed behind them shortly. I overheard Sergey stammering to get something out to one of his team. His dark gray suit only made his soft, boyish face look younger. Nervously looking around as he entered the Fulton Market Building to compete for the world title, Sergey looked more like a kid with a fake ID trying to get past a bouncer into a strip club. But then, there is something lurid about a chess championship's agonizing, drawn-out pressure inevitably stripping naked two psyches before all the world, scars and all. Carlsen had always been vocal about how much he enjoyed above all else making wriggling, pinned insects of his adversaries, holding them at toy gunpoint until they walked off a plank or into an open grave. Karjakin had become the youngest grandmaster in history already more than half his lifetime ago: it had taken him far longer than he'd planned to arrive where he was. Now that he was here, could he live up to the phenomenal potential he'd demonstrated as a boy? What if he couldn't? Would this opportunity ever arrive again, or would he just be a trampled footnote in the legacy of Magnus Carlsen?

A wiry photographer in his late thirties with a shaved head spoke Russian while grabbing as many shots as he could of the challenger. After Sergey disappeared into the VIP section, the photographer bent over his camera, making disgruntled faces while inspecting what he'd gotten. I approached him.

"Interesting morning," he said in a thick Russian accent. "No Zuckerberg or Bill Gates as advertised, but we have the Kremlin here and Woody Harrelson from *Cheers* to make the ceremonial first move."

The photographer, Misha Friedman, was shooting the match for the *New York Times*. He was originally from Moldova. After the collapse of the Soviet Union, fourteen-year-old Misha had arrived in Brooklyn with his parents. They couldn't speak English and had no money. He attended Edward R. Murrow High School, where he was a member of its émigré powerhouse chess team. All members had arrived from Eastern Bloc countries, and every player on the Murrow team was rated considerably above 2000. Misha wasn't the star of the team, he told me, but he was good enough to get legitimate notes to skip regular classes. With barely enough money to allow them to travel, the team members—who were accustomed to state support back in the Soviet Union—won the national championships all three years Misha competed.

I walked with Misha past security into the VIP section. It was early afternoon and the bartender was already serving drinks at a pretty rapid clip. We sat down on a couch.

"Is this the first time you've photographed Magnus?" I asked.

"No," Misha said. "In August of 2013, just before Magnus won the world championship for the first time, I flew to Norway to shoot him for *Time* magazine. Magnus had just been named one of their Most Influential People in the World. He was getting real attention for the first time. His people promised me an exclusive at a resort called Kragerø in southern Norway, right on the North Sea coast. He was preparing, but for the media day it was set up like a circus. He had a kind of handler working for him, who worked with high-profile Norwegian athletes. That guy and the owner of the resort were both former beach volleyball players who played at a high level. They were these absolutely enormous Viking men who dwarfed Magnus, who isn't small by any means. For the photo ops they wanted Magnus to play all kinds of sports for the cameras—volleyball, tennis, golf. He was playing with this handler and the resort owner, and it was obvious both of these guys were much better at the things Magnus was doing. But they had to let him win. Magnus might get upset if he lost and maybe not practise his chess afterward. He was moody and childish the whole day. They were trying to promote Magnus but also the resort at the same time. The photo shoot was just designed to be PR for the Norwegian media."

"Could you tell he was someone special right away?" I asked.

"He treated us like shit. After the photo-op bullshit, they gave me maybe five minutes with him alone. He was eating pizza and watching funny chess videos. Magnus seemed much younger than his age. Around that time, *Vice* came out with an article called 'Magnus Carlsen Is Kind of a Dick.' He *was* kind of a dick."

"How so?"

"Do you like most eleven-year-old movie stars? Do you think Macaulay Culkin would have been fun to spend time with after *Home Alone*? All Magnus has ever done is play chess all day every day of his life. Who's the most famous person Norway has ever had? Edvard Munch?"

"I dunno. Karl Ove Knausgård?"

"It's a pretty anonymous place for most of the world. After the world championship, some European magazines were naming Magnus one of the sexiest men of the year and that sort of thing. *Chess* and *sex symbol* are not words that usually go together."

I noticed a stately older man lumber a little uneasily into the room and become quickly surrounded by well-wishers. Even a little hunched over he was still well over six feet, dressed neatly in a vest and tie, with a jacket hung over his forearm. Someone asked for his photograph and he reflexively adjusted his glasses, ran a quick hand over his full head of white hair, and scrunched his goatee. He saturated the room with his charm and warmth immediately.

"Dr. Frank Brady," Misha said. "Fischer's biographer. He was president of the Marshall Chess Club in the West Village too. You'll love him."

But before Misha could introduce me, we were hijacked by a tall, middle-aged man with a slightly grown-out brush cut, wearing a blazer. He forcefully grabbed Misha's hand and stared into his eyes for a few moments with the longing and strange, vaguely sinister intensity of a 1950s door-to-door vacuum salesman, before finally introducing himself in a reedy, high-pitched Nordic accent as a grandmaster.

"I was a child world champion also," he said.

After he asked who Misha was covering the event for, he took out a notebook and requested our contact information so we could stay in touch. Misha and I both stood in stunned silence. Then he noticed Brady, lost all interest in us, tucked his notebook into his pocket to reset the trap, and bull-rushed the old man, who nearly spilled his freshly ordered Diet Coke over himself.

"Where else are GMs supposed to network?" Misha said. "For three weeks this place is a gold mine for him."

About a month earlier, at a rally in Ambridge, Pennsylvania, Donald Trump was bashing America's trade deals when, in a characteristic Trumpian non sequitur, he also took a swipe at the country's chess prowess: "We will stop the disastrous Trans-Pacific Partnership, which would be almost as bad as NAFTA. Nothing could be as bad. But we'll stop it. And we'll make deals. But this is a complex deal with many countries. You have to see the arrows all over the place. Once you sign it, it's 5,000 pages, more than that long. Once you sign it, it's a mess. . . . You have to be like a grand chessmaster, and we don't have any of them."

Not quite. At the time, America in fact had 90 chess grandmasters, the third highest total in the world after Germany (91) and Russia (234).

It was in Russia that the term *grandmaster* originated. In

1914, Czar Nicholas II hosted a chess tournament in Saint Petersburg. The best chess players in the world attended. Germany's mathematician and philosopher Emanuel Lasker, the defending world champion, would come from behind and narrowly defeat Cuban José Raúl Capablanca. (Lasker's reign as world champion would last twenty-seven years.) Legends Alexander Alekhine, Siegbert Tarrasch, and American Frank Marshall would finish third, fourth, and fifth respectively. After Lasker's victory, Nicholas II held a banquet and declared the group "grandmasters of chess" and history's first original players to hold that title.

Today there are nearly 1,600 chess grandmasters. And it seemed like just about all of them were there at the Fulton Market. It wasn't hard to see why. Here they were not eccentrics, misfits, or dealt with as objects of curiosity, as they might have been in the outside world. Instead they were regarded with the esteem afforded brilliant people who crossed a Rubicon and joined the intellectual equivalent of the Knights of the Round Table. They were glittering jewels encrusting the hoisted-across-fifteen-hundred-years-of-history crown of the game of kings.

A common feature emerged with the many grandmasters I would meet over those two weeks. Each time I was introduced to one, they almost invariably mentioned their title immediately after offering their name. It was never prompted, and I was never quite sure what the appropriate response was. Chess, I discovered, is an endeavor almost preternaturally obsessed with status, hierarchy, title, rank, pecking order—with every member defined by their rating. The more they associate their identity with this valuation of their worth, the more those outside this domain seem to gnaw and inspire some measure of defensiveness. It's a lot like Mensa. I've never met any exceedingly bright people concerned with Mensa who aren't existing *members* of Mensa—which invariably leads to some defensiveness about exactly what that achievement means *beyond* being a member of Mensa. So the chess elite strolled about the room with a self-conscious combination of swagger and desperation.

Their desperation was compounded by the fact that while the staggering dilution of the title's original significance has expanded the membership tremendously, achieving the distinction in no way insures a passport to economic viability for any but a select few. Several grandmasters I would talk to over the course of these two weeks assured me that only about thirty players could make a living exclusively playing chess. So, like the vast majority of all artists, to survive they had to teach. In this way, the championship served as a sort of job fair, where grandmasters like our pushy Nordic friend came to find students.

Of which there were plenty. Misha and I had moved from the VIP couch to one of the tables to play while we waited for the first game to start. A bushy-haired Asian child with deep-set inquisitive eyes and a quick smile drowning in adorable cheeks approached us and inspected the board with his father standing behind him. He was dressed in a shiny blue US Chess Federation team tracksuit. His name, Awonder Liang, was stitched over his heart.

"How old are you?" I asked.

"Thirteen," he said.

"How long have you been playing?"

"Since I was five."

His father, Will Liang, informed me that Awonder had won the under-eight and under-ten World Youth Chess Championships in

2011 and 2013, in Brazil and the United Arab Emirates, respectively. They lived in Madison, Wisconsin. Awonder was one of the most promising chess prodigies in the world. He had beaten his first grandmaster at the age of nine—the youngest player in history ever to do so.

"If Sergey can't beat Magnus, will we be seeing you going after the crown soon enough?" I asked.

"Hopefully," Awonder said cheerfully. "I'll have to see how it goes."

Just then, a mime with a face painted white stole Awonder's attention with an orb rolling around his tuxedo. And my attention was stolen by the sight of Woody Harrelson in the corner playing a game with himself. Harrelson was there to make the honorary first move.

"Did you think they paid Woody as much as the *Entourage* guy at the Plaza last night?" I asked Misha.

"No," he said. "Woody actually loves chess. He's hooked. Nobody paid him anything to come."

Finally, the giant flat-screens spread out across the VIP section mercifully ceased showing the endless loop of sponsors, and up popped a digital chessboard alongside a video feed of the actual rosewood-and-maple championship board, containing opposing armies of ebonized boxwood (each piece equipped with a sensor and all designed by architect Daniel Weil to be proportioned to the pitch of the façade of the Parthenon), led by two three-and-three-quarter-inch, 2.2-ounce kings, and a lone maroon DGT 2010 official chess clock. The two chairs where the champion and challenger might spend over a hundred man-hours sitting? The

Baird Bonded Leather Managers Chair, appearing more suited to the deck of *Star Trek*'s *Enterprise*, retails from a Staples office supply store for $270.

There was an eerie, haunting simplicity to the most important sixty-four squares in the world. The imaginary battlefield occupied by two make-believe armies, the board was shielded behind a thick pane of mirrored, one-way, soundproof glass, mounted on a plain table, flanked by two clipboards. Two young men, the finest chess players the world had at this particular moment in time, brought from thousands of miles away, were finally drawing within inches of one another to silently wage war for the next three weeks. This board was their canvas on which to simultaneously create and destroy a masterpiece in the unique fashion only chess affords its most sublime artists.

I was hushed by security as I walked through the black curtains to enter the dark, sideshow tent–like viewing gallery to wait out the last fleeting moments before the beginning of the first world championship to be held in New York City since September 11, 1995, when Garry Kasparov faced off against Viswanathan Anand on the 107th floor of the south tower of the World Trade Center. A spooky purple glow shone through the one-way mirror onto the faces of perhaps fifty eager children and impatient businessmen as Karjakin entered the room first, walking stiffly. He sat down, unbuttoned his blazer to allow for a deep breath, and leaned back in his chair. As Karjakin began adjusting his black pieces to center them on their squares, we watched as the ritual seemed to soothe him. Suddenly Carlsen arrived at the table and offered his hand to the challenger, and the photographers unleashed a last rapid fire of bursting light into the room. Carlsen seemed poised and relaxed as he reached for a bottle of the Norwegian sponsor's water. Organizers posed for one last photo op with Woody Harrelson as he made the first ceremonial move on behalf of Carlsen's white pawn. Karjakin quickly responded by bringing out his knight. As photographers and organizers made their way out of the room, Carlsen confounded experts' predictions about his opening strategy by bringing out his bishop.

There was some laughter from chess aficionados in the viewing gallery.

"A Trompowsky for President Trump," a Russian voice snickered from the corner of the room.

Carlsen had used the Trompowsky three years earlier at the Tal Memorial against former world champion Vladimir Kramnik and won, but was this method of attack more a phonetic wink at Donald Trump? His father, Henrik, was interviewed soon after and seemed to think so. Carlsen had admitted on Norwegian television the previous March that he was a "big fan of Donald Trump. . . . Trump is incredibly good at finding opponents' weaknesses."

On this day, Magnus would not find any of Sergey's weaknesses. The first game ended after nearly four hours when both agreed to a draw after the forty-second move. When a reporter asked him if the Trompowsky was in any way a nod to President Trump, Carlsen grinned mischievously. "A little bit."

# 4

# STILL SEARCHING FOR
# BOBBY FISCHER

It was just over four miles from the site of the championship to 560
Lincoln Place, apartment Q, where, on a rainy day in 1949, Bobby
Fischer's sister first brought up a plastic chess set, with red and
black squares and hollow pieces, that she bought for a buck from
the local candy store to keep her lonely brother company just after
his sixth birthday. It was the first time Fischer had seen a chessboard in his life. Instantly the fuse was lit. For Fischer, the encounter with the chessboard catalyzed his place in the world. Soon he
would be capable of some of the most biblically majestic and strange
acts—on and off the board—that history had ever witnessed. The
ensuing years would see him go from America's Cold War hero,
celebrated on the covers of *Time* and *Life* and *Newsweek*, to a fu-
gitive from justice, owing to his insistence on violating American

economic sanctions and playing in Yugoslavia, ultimately becoming a Unabomber-like character who removed his dental work to forestall presumed CIA surveillance, raged publicly as a virulent anti-Semite and Holocaust denier, and following the 9/11 attacks called into a Philippines radio station to say, "This is all wonderful news. It's time for the fucking US to get their heads kicked in. It's time to finish off the US once and for all. . . . I want to see the US *wiped out*."

A twenty-nine-year-old Fischer told Mike Wallace, during an interview for *60 Minutes* that aired on April 9, 1972, "I remember the first thing they [the Russian media] ever wrote about me was that I was a talented player . . . but all this publicity I was getting and all the attention cannot fail to have a harmful effect on my personality development. And sure enough, a few months later, I was a rotten person already in their press. I was doing this, I was doing that, I was conceited, you know. This was before they ever even knew anything about me personally."

Of course, by design, it was hard to know anything about Fischer personally. "He lives alone," Wallace reported, "always in hotel rooms that seem barely larger than chessboards. The television set is his window on the world. . . . It is almost the only company he keeps. A lot of the time he won't even answer his telephone. He's shy. Suspicious of strangers. It took us nearly six months to persuade him to sit for this television portrait. . . . He has no advisers, no coaches, no manager. He doesn't really trust anyone's advice. In a sense, his most reliable friends are the pieces on the board. His strategies in life as in chess are mysterious and his own."

Forty years later, in another *60 Minutes* profile, Bob Simon asked Magnus about Fischer's descent into madness.

"Do you ever think about that?"

"Yes, I do," Magnus said. "You know, when I was watching the recent film about Bobby Fischer, I was thinking, 'Is this going to be me in a few years?' I don't think that's going to happen, but it made me think a little bit that I have to be aware of this at least."

In order to answer my editor's questions about Magnus, I felt like I had to better understand Fischer. I read as many books and saw as many documentaries about him as I could—watched everything I could find on YouTube. The most revealing were the three interviews Fischer did on *The Dick Cavett Show*.

In the lead-up to 1972 world championship, Cavett asked Fischer, "What's the moment of pleasure for you? Is it when you see the guy in trouble? Where's the greatest pleasure that corresponds to hitting the home run in baseball?"

"Uh, the greatest pleasure?" Fischer stroked his chin, pondering. "Huh. Well, when you break his ego. That's where it's at. You know?"

Fischer then smiled sadistically before offering Cavett a face worthy of the Coney Island clown horrifyingly come to life. Fischer giggled uncontrollably as the studio audience gasped.

"Really?" Cavett asked.

"Yeah." Fischer giggled some more, this time with the audience joining him.

"And when does that occur? When he sees that he's finished?"

"Yeah, you know. He sees it's coming and, uh, breaks up all inside."

Later that same year, after winning the title from Boris Spassky in Reykjavík on September 1 in front of one of the largest global television audiences in history, Fischer came back on Cavett's show for the final time.

The high school dropout from Brooklyn, who had mastered one of the world's most complicated intellectual endeavors on his own from inside his small Crown Heights apartment, had symbolically taken on and brought down the mighty Soviet Union. The win was as big a victory in the Cold War as the Apollo moon landing had been three years earlier. Fischer's victories at the chessboard in Iceland were daily front-page news in the *New York Times*, and Walter Cronkite informed America about Vietnam and the Watergate scandal only after he offered updates from Reykjavík. After Fischer took the crown, chess became so popular in the United States that inmates at New York's Rikers Island jail were photographed reaching through the bars to play on boards placed on tables outside their cells.

Fischer, wearing a burgundy suit, received a roaring ovation when he arrived onstage. Cavett's other guest was actor Tony Randall, from the TV hit *The Odd Couple*.

"The *New York Times* reviewer," Randall said, referencing Pulitzer Prize winner Harold Schonberg, who covered both music and chess for the paper, "wrote that you are a merciless sadist without feelings for others, whose only wish is to destroy your opponent. Is that true?"

Fischer smiled coyly.

"No," he said.

"Crushing a man's ego," Cavett jumped in. "Was there that moment? A *specific* moment?"

"I'll tell you," Fischer said with a grin, his eyes beginning to gleam with the casual menace of Rasputin. "That was the one

thing I didn't really enjoy about this match. Because I never felt he gave up. He never just . . . *collapsed*. He tried to make a fight of it to the end."

"So you never really had that moment?" Cavett asked.

"Just at the very end," Fischer said. "The last game. The last couple of games. I started to feel him getting a little despondent. I kinda started to feel it a *little* bit. But not the real full measure, you know, that I *like*."

"But you're not a merciless sadist who likes to destroy your opponents," Randall said.

"Of course not," Cavett said.

The three men and the crowd laughed.

I wrote to Cavett asking if he would speak to me. He had gotten a fair bit of shit over his fondness for Fischer, especially when in 2008 he wrote a column in the *New York Times* referring to Fischer's death as "among this year's worst news." He mailed me recordings of all three of their conversations but said he no longer wished to discuss their relationship.

I reached out to a few other people who had encountered Fischer personally. One was the author Gay Talese.

In 1957, a twenty-five-year-old Talese had been hired to work at the *New York Times* sports desk after getting out of the army. He was sniffing around New York for the stories and characters that would soon make him one of the most legendary journalists of the twentieth century. Only a few months before, a thirteen-year-old Fischer had made headlines around the world for a game he played at the Marshall Chess Club in New York's West Village. Fischer sacrificed his queen on the seventeenth move of his

game against twenty-six-year-old Donald Byrne, one of the top players in the country. Time was running out for Fischer, and when Byrne took the piece, many in the room thought the cocky kid had cracked under the pressure and hung the most important piece on the board. Twenty-four moves later, after five hours, all the room of spectators finally saw that Bobby's masterpiece was a paint-by-numbers he'd seen a mile off. Even Byrne smiled after being mated, well aware he had been on the losing end of a historic game that would soon be crowned "the Game of the Century."

Hearing word of this, Talese wrote one of the first profiles of Fischer. He first found the boy sipping a Coke inside an air-conditioned bar near the Manhattan Chess Club. Fischer confessed that he used to cry whenever he lost, but before long he hardly ever lost. "Players with Fischer's talent come along only once in a century," the Manhattan Chess Club president Maurice J. Kasper told Talese. But there was already gossip that the genius was troubled. Fischer's mother told Talese she spent four years trying to get her son away from the game. She thought it would be too much strain on him. Fischer admitted that he had been "addicted" to chess since the age of six. "Always serious," Talese wrote in his piece, "he peers grimly down at the chessboard as if the fate of mankind hinged on his next move. . . . Genius being as unpredictable as it is astounding, the future of the remarkable Bobby is anyone's guess. . . . The young genius had no explanation for his genius. He simply ordered another Coke."

I met Talese at a café near his Upper East Side home to discuss his encounter with Fischer.

"You ever see Fischer after that first meeting?" I asked.

"Nope," he said. He seemed more interested in impaling his cherry pastry with a fork than in answering my questions.

"Never wanted to follow up?" I asked.

"Never did," he said. "Listen, I told you I was happy to meet and talk, but I don't want any homework on this. I'm too old and I'm already late on a book I owe my publisher. This was sixty fuckin' years ago. There was something just as spooky as there was special about Bobby, even back then."

Eventually I found someone who'd encountered Fischer and had some insight to offer: Errol Morris, arguably the greatest documentary filmmaker who ever lived. Like Fischer, Morris spent some time in Brooklyn growing up. Before his third birthday, his father, a doctor, died suddenly of a heart attack. Growing up, Morris was surrounded by evidence of a father who wasn't there. Not entirely surprising, then, that this brilliant mind would spend a lifetime obsessed with conducting investigations—first as a private investigator and then as a filmmaker.

"It just so happens that the psychiatrist that I saw when I was very young also saw Fischer," Morris told me over the phone from his Cambridge, Massachusetts, home. "I remember bumping into him and his mother. I was seeing a psychiatrist as early as the late fifties. I'm five years younger than Bobby. I haven't thought of him in a long time. I got into a terrible fight about him once, when that movie *Searching for Bobby Fischer* had just come out in the early nineties. My son was six or seven, like the hero in the film. I disliked the movie immensely, while everyone else seemed to really like it. I basically hated the argument the film made. The argument was as if the kid had a choice. The choice is, would you rather be the greatest chess player in the world or perhaps the greatest chess player who ever lived, versus an all-around kind of *citizen of the community*. I thought the question itself was ridiculous. Also, I knew how I would answer the question, even though it's not really a question. It's not like, you know, would you rather be Franz Kafka, or would you rather be John Q. Citizen. And if you ask me—"

"Errol," I said, "I'd like to ask you—"

"*I'd rather be Franz fucking Kafka!* I'd rather be Bobby Fischer. And that goes with knowing that these people lived tortured lives. Having said that, there *is* no choice here. It's not as if you have some kind of smorgasbord where you can select one from column A and one from column B. You're in so many ways indentured to yourself and who you are and what your obsessions are, and what your talents are. I thought *Searching for Bobby Fischer*, the movie, got it all wrong. Bobby Fischer had no choice but to be Bobby Fischer. It's not as though he could sit down one day and say, 'I think I'll be a normal human being because it's much easier to live that way.' That was not an option, a box that you could check, an alternative. He had to be Bobby Fischer. And he was cursed with this endowment of extraordinary ability. It's not about discipline. That's not what is at issue. I've realized from many gifted prodigies I've encountered—and I've known a number of them in my day—particularly in music, that there was no discipline involved at all. They were all compulsive. They were obsessive. They couldn't *not* do what they were doing."

"This is a fascinating point," I said. "We always say people who get to the top sacrificed so much, yet I can never figure out what they sacrificed. Weren't they the only ones who didn't have to sacrifice anything and got to do the thing they loved more than anything else *all* the fucking time? Everyone around them sure had to sacrifice to support them and their dream. But what did they sacrifice?"

"Nobody had to tell these people who get to the top, 'You sit and play at the piano or the chessboard for twenty hours a day, you fucker!'" Morris said. "It's none of that. I went to the music school in France and there are all kinds of prodigies there. Real prodigies. I remember this eleven-year-old kid who later won the Van Cliburn competition. And his goal was to learn to play Mendelssohn's Variations. His parents had to *restrict* the amount he could play the piano every day. That's how this stuff really works. And to have *Searching for Bobby Fischer* lecture me on the nature of prodigies and the choices available to prodigies, it was dishonest to say the least. Bobby Fischer had no choice! If it was put to me, I would take the choice to be bat-shit crazy and to do something extraordinarily well."

Errol Morris wasn't a chess player.

"I played when I was kid," he told me. "I was never ever good at chess."

But there was another filmmaker who'd grown up in New York and *loved* to play. In the 1950s, a twentysomething photographer for *Look* magazine named Stanley Kubrick who was just starting to dabble in motion pictures could often be found playing chess down in Greenwich Village's Washington Square Park. "I would go there about twelve o'clock and stay there until midnight," he said in 1966 in a rare interview he gave to Jeremy Bernstein of *The New Yorker*. "In the summer it was marvelous. In the daytime you'd get a table by the shade and at nighttime you'd get a table by the light."

Kubrick was famous for playing chess on the set of his films. In 1964, when he clashed with George C. Scott while working on *Dr. Strangelove*, Kubrick found out Scott fancied himself a strong chess player and immediately challenged him to a game. After Kubrick soundly thrashed Scott on the board, the actor became much more malleable to Kubrick's direction and ideas.

The same year *2001: A Space Odyssey* was released, Kubrick spoke with *Playboy*, explaining how chess had greatly informed his approach to filmmaking:

"Among a great many other things that chess teaches you is to control the initial excitement you feel when you see something that looks good. It trains you to think before grabbing, and to think just as objectively when you're in trouble. When you're making a film you have to make most of your decisions on the run, and there is a tendency to always shoot from the hip. It takes more discipline than you might imagine to think, even for thirty seconds, in the noisy, confusing, high-pressure atmosphere of a film set. But a few seconds' thought can often prevent a serious mistake being made about something that looks good at first glance. With respect to films, chess is more useful preventing you from making mistakes than giving you ideas. Ideas come spontaneously and the discipline required to evaluate and put them to use tends to be the real work."

In a 2010 essay on Kubrick and chess for the *New York Review of Books*, Jeremy Bernstein wrote of how he and the director, who'd become friendly, watched together at Kubrick's London home the *60 Minutes* profile of Fischer. Which led me to wonder if Kubrick had ever crossed paths with Fischer back when he was playing in the Village. So I got in touch with his eighty-five-year-old widow,

Christiane, who lives in London. She couldn't remember anything about Fischer, but we did talk for a bit over the phone about her late husband's relationship to the game.

"He learned as a child and was hooked very early," she said with a laugh. "It *ruined* him in school. He never paid any attention in school and just played chess. He cheated the rest of the time. Later he played chess with computers. He was in danger of being swallowed up by it. He felt it was compulsive and an addiction as powerful as smoking. Losing days or weeks, he knew he was in danger. But he was careful to not give in and focused on his work with films."

Around the same time Kubrick was shooting for *Look*, Scottish photographer Harry Benson was living in London and working for the *Daily Express* newspaper. In 1964, Benson was supposed to go to Uganda for a story on the country's recent independence from British rule, but his editor at the paper had a last-minute change of plans and instead sent him to Paris to photograph a young rock-and-roll band called the Beatles. It was on that assignment that Benson captured their famous hotel room pillow fight—helping launch his own career as well as that of the band. Benson has gotten up close and photographed every American president since Eisenhower. Odds were, if you were anybody or anything making a dent in the culture in the second half of the twentieth century, Benson had flown around the world in order to take your picture. "A great photograph can never happen again," Benson once said of his aim with taking pictures. On April 4, 1968, in Memphis, he heard Martin Luther King Jr. had been shot and rushed to the Lorraine Motel only to find the police had just left. The motel room's door was slightly open. One of the civil rights leaders, Hosea Williams, was sobbing inside while wringing towels of something strange into a jar. Benson asked him what it was. "This is Martin's blood," Williams told him. Two months later, Benson was six feet away from Robert F. Kennedy, who had just finished a speech at the Ambassador Hotel in Los Angeles when another assassin's bullet was fatally fired. Five other people were shot immediately around Benson.

In late 1971, Benson was assigned by *Life* magazine to cover Bobby Fischer after another photographer dropped out at the last minute. After Fischer's victory against Tigran Vartanovich Petrosian in the 1971 Candidates Tournament, he had earned the right to challenge Boris Spassky for the world title. Benson flew to meet Fischer at his hotel in Buenos Aires at around one in the morning. Fischer invited Benson to join him on a walk. Fischer brought along a pocket chess set. Benson didn't even know how to play.

Benson photographed Fischer playing chess with children in the park, at amusement parks on his own, riding horses, smelling roses, being licked by a collie. The intimacy and vulnerability Fischer offered in these photos was unique. And as America grappled with the Watergate scandal and fifty-seven thousand American deaths and counting in Vietnam, Fischer's looming Cold War battle against the Soviet Union began to overshadow everything on the news. Benson's portrait of Fischer made the cover of *Life* on November 12, 1971.

Harry Benson invited me to speak with him at the apartment

he shares with his wife and business manager, Gigi, on Manhattan's Upper East Side. Even at eighty-seven, Benson still wears his collar popped, has a full head of messy white hair and amused black eyes under bushy eyebrows. His life's work hangs on most of the walls of his apartment: President Ronald Reagan pulling a horse out of a barn, Hillary and Bill Clinton lying together in a hammock, Muhammad Ali's fist mock-striking the Beatles' heads as if tipping over a row of dominos, a white cop smoking a cigarette while the African American that he's just killed lies sprawled out before him, Frank Sinatra and Mia Farrow in masks at Truman Capote's Black and White Ball at the Plaza.

"I don't know anything about chess," Benson said in his melodic, singsong voice, after taking a sip from a can of Coke and petting his seventeen-year-old dog Tilly. "But I've been a photographer my entire adult life. I've photographed a lot of people. Bobby Fischer is the most extraordinary man I've ever met and the most interesting person I've ever photographed."

"How can that be?" I said. "Especially when you don't even *care* about chess."

"I'm really not sure." Benson shrugged innocently. "But it's true."

"But how can anyone understand someone who has photographed every president since *Eisenhower*, seeing power so up close, that a chess player—"

"Bobby was very powerful too."

"In what way?"

"Just the way he had about him. He didn't care what anybody thought. He really didn't."

"Did you like him?"

"Yes, I did. I was one of the few people that liked him. It's very hard to be critical of someone that allows you to do your job and gives you total and complete access. Bobby did that with me."

"Why did he do that?"

"He liked the idea of being a big shot. He never identified with chess people. He didn't like them. He identified with jocks. We never talked about chess. I knew nothing. When he trained for Iceland at Grossinger's, he trained like an athlete and I photographed him during that time."

Fischer agreed to allow Benson access while he trained in the Catskill Mountains resort in upstate New York for the chess world championship. Fischer flatly refused to even talk to any other outsider. He liked training where Rocky Marciano and other boxing legends had prepared for boxing title matches. He ran in the mornings, played table tennis, punched a heavy bag, swam laps, skipped rope, and held his breath underwater to improve his stamina and nerves under pressure. At night he went back to his hotel room, put on a visor, and studied chess for endless hours on his own. He allowed Benson to document all of it.

"He was playing against the best in Iceland and he was alone," Benson said. "It made him feel like a prizefighter alone in the ring. He didn't want anybody's advice. He didn't think of himself as an intellectual. More of an athlete. He didn't like the way chess people looked."

Benson spent the entire summer of 1972 in Iceland to cover Fischer's match against Spassky. At first it seemed as if Fischer was content not to show up at all. The opening ceremony took place without him. It was only after the prize fund was doubled and Henry Kissinger called from the White House to plead with him that Fischer relented and got on a plane. Late on the night Fischer arrived, he knocked on Benson's door and invited him on a walk.

"Iceland was the land of the midnight sun, as they say. It was never dark. We drove a few miles outside Reykjavík to the lava fields and walked for hours. Sometimes he talked. Sometimes he was quiet. I took some of my favorite shots of him on a boat at three in the morning. Dead of night but not dark in the least. He threw a blanket over himself and was sitting on the edge of the boat. All his isolation is just right there. Naked. He had been alone so much of his life. There was always only chess. We're talking about someone with totally nonexistent social skills. He was always pleasant with me. Fun sense of humor. But very, very isolated."

"What was he like on that boat?" I asked.

Benson sighed.

"Free. Free. *Free*. Nobody bothering him. Bobby felt that chess for him was the same as for a fighter. He was going in there alone. It wasn't a team sport he was in. And, you know, he didn't want to just beat his opponents either. He wanted to tear people apart and humiliate them. Really bring them down. His idea was to tear them apart."

"It sounds like you're talking about Muhammad Ali," I said.

"I covered most of Ali's career. Bobby and Ali had similarities. Their eyes, for example. Both Ali's and Fischer's eyes were like snakes'. Ali never took his eye off his opponent. Never took his eye off."

"Did you see immense cruelty in Fischer's eyes?" I asked.

"Yeah. I did. He didn't want to let his opponents go. His

attitude was, 'You're going to pay for this. How dare you be in front of me.' Ali had the same look. They both watched everything in their opponents. Fischer watched everything, saw every detail anywhere in the room going on. He was just such a wonderful, wonderful character. There's no characters like him anymore, or Ali. Where is a Truman Capote anymore? We're short of these characters. I don't really see many people right now that are on the same class, the same status, you know?"

"What do you remember most from Fischer beating Spassky in Iceland?" I asked.

"Just before the twenty-first game, I was supposed to photograph Spassky before he went to the hall to play. I went to his hotel and found him walking in the lobby. When I got up close he turned to me and said, 'There is a new world champion. His name is Robert James Fischer.' He turned around and said he was going for a walk. I rushed back to the Loftleidir hotel and banged on Bobby's door to give him the news."

Benson laughed.

"He was suspicious! He went over to a chessboard in the bedroom and looked over the position of the game. Then Bobby went over to the hall to hear the announcement. The *New York Times* reported the next day on the front page of the paper that Bobby first heard the news he was champion from my having telephoned him. They got that wrong."

"And then Bobby disappeared," I said. "Did you see that coming?"

"He could have made millions of dollars if he kept going, but he didn't. He didn't trust people. Didn't trust this. Didn't trust that. He could have been a very rich man. There was only one of him. He said that chess was nothing without him. He was right."

Gigi brought in a pot of tea and a tray of cookies. Benson bit off a corner of a cookie and gave Tilly some attention for a minute.

"When was the last time you saw him?" I asked.

"Saw him in Los Angeles ten years before he died. A long time ago. I'd seen him a few times in LA before that. He was involved with a church that took all his money."

"Did you see him as a friend or as work?" I asked.

"I've never gotten close to anybody. In my business? There's a lot of reasons for that."

"When I look at the way Fischer is looking into your camera at you, it's pretty clear there's a profound level of trust and a strange connection."

"There could be a connection."

Benson leaned down and stroked Tilly's chin.

"Bobby was in a dark place all his life," Benson said. "He really was sad."

Gigi brought over a few collections of her husband's photographs. Benson opened the book up to the middle, and there Michael Jackson stood at the entrance to his bedroom, guarded by the statue of a Boy Scout and a Girl Scout reaching over with their hands high above their heads to create an arch.

"That was the first time he ever let a photographer into his bedroom. Huge throne inside there where he let me take a photo of him sitting in it."

Benson turned the page and Marlon Brando appeared. "Piece of shit. Not a pleasant man. Fat and—*shit*."

He turned another page. John Lennon. "Halfway through

that first week when they were hitting America, it was sensational to be around them. Fischer mania, in a way, was like that. In a way it was."

Benson turned the page and Andy Warhol's face was shielded behind a camera as Benson took his picture.

"Warhol would have enjoyed Bobby," Benson said. "They would have enjoyed each other. Warhol is another class of character we haven't got anymore. They're all gone, really. Bobby, Andy, Truman—so many great characters. Who has replaced them?"

"You don't see any?" I asked.

"Well . . ." Benson shrugged and reached for another cookie. He turned the page with his free hand, and there was Donald Trump feigning the pose of a boxer atop the Trump Tower with the New York skyline behind him.

"When was the first time you photographed him?" I said.

"Forty years ago," Benson said. "He was around thirty. I've known him for years."

"You're friends?" I asked.

"I think he's *terrible*. I think he's awful. I feel sorry for America."

"How many years after meeting him did you suspect he would run for president?"

"*Years?* Five *minutes* after meeting him I knew he would run for president. From the very beginning it was obvious he would want that. And now he's won and it's not good. You could tell the second you met him, all Trump wanted to do was take over. It was like meeting Hitler in that way. Just wanted total power. I hate to say it, but Bobby probably would have voted for Trump. Even with that being the case, Bobby was somebody I would have liked to have said goodbye to. You know, people are in your life and the next thing you know, they're dead. I would like to have one more chance to pass a little bit of the day with Bobby one more time. I'm very sad that I'll never see him again. I knew him at the best time in his life. Now you can't write a word about chess without remembering him."

# 5

# THE HUSTLERS

On the morning of the second game, Magnus, hair slicked back, entered the glassed-in, soundproof shipping container–size room. Two aging arbiters followed behind him. Carlsen sat down and entered his information on the score sheet before carefully adjusting his black chess pieces on the board. He gazed around the room for his opponent and, not finding him, instead discovered his reflection in the one-way mirror. He stared for a few moments before violently rubbing his eyes with one hand. Then, leaning over to bury his face in his palm, he took deep breaths. Carlsen removed his hand and searched the room once more for his opponent. Finally he sank back in his chair and folded his arms. The photographers were let into the room. Magnus turned away from them and sank his cheek into his collar as their flashes exploded. The expression on his face resembled that of an animal recognizing there was no escape from a sprung trap fastened to its leg.

Karjakin arrived soon after, behind the throng of cameras, and reached out his hand to Carlsen, who remained seated, like Captain Kirk in his USS *Enterprise* chair. When he was seated himself, Karjakin reached out over the board and bent his wrists to lower his delicate hands over his white pieces with his fingers pressed together, resembling a pelican's beak bobbing at fish, as he went after each of their heads. Carlsen turned away from his opponent and the cameras and for a few moments leaned against his shoulder and closed his eyes like a dozing child. Karjakin folded his arms and tensely looked away from the cameras as well, staring off into the mirror while nervously trying to regain control of his breathing.

Each game was to begin with a ceremonial celebrity first-move photo op. For the first game it had been Woody Harrelson. Today it was . . . the CEO of PhosAgro, the Russian fertilizer company sponsoring the event. He lumbered into the room and Karjakin deferentially informed him of the first move he wished to make. Soon enough, nearly everyone but the two arbiters left the premises and the two young men were alone with only the board between them.

Watching chess played up close, at the highest level, is like sitting down in a theater for three weeks and watching back-to-back-to-back every Andy Warhol film where the camera never moves. When are we allowed to stare at anyone, undisturbed, for such duration, aside from our children sleeping? As they struggle against fatigue, nerves, anxiety, distraction, you watch each man's essential light fade like a boat being consumed by the horizon. You feel less like a spectator of a sport than a nurse in an asylum. It's astounding to watch up close the gradual and brutal effects hours of sustained concentration inflict on chess players at the world's highest level. There they are, trapped like conjoined twins in solitary confinement, sometimes breaking away from the board, seemingly to make sure invisible walls aren't closing in on them. The sight of Carlsen and Karjakin caged and steadying themselves for possibly two or three solid *days*' worth of play yet to come over the coming weeks at the board was almost as nauseating as any bloody, grueling prizefight I'd witnessed. The previous day, before the championship's opening move, the two men had looked years younger than their actual ages. By the end of the day, with their faces falling, they looked ten years older. A night of sleep had only helped a little.

After standing in front of the executioner's window for a few minutes, I wandered around the floor. It was a Saturday, and so with no school there were even more kids there than the day before. In addition, New York schools had given students free tickets to that day's game. Chessboards were scattered all over the space. In every direction you looked kids were playing. Swimming in their sweaters. Fiddling with their braces. A hundred brains squeezed by the vise of two hands jammed against temples. And it wasn't just kids. It was all ages and colors, men and women, boys and girls—all helpless to resist the same addiction, the same itch that wouldn't let them pass an abandoned chessboard without molesting it. Pieces were captured and piled up on either side of the boards like jackpot silver dollars spilling from slots. For a second it felt like I was back in a Vegas casino showroom during the lead-up to fight week—truly the eighth circle of hell.

Yet there was a distinct difference. The chess players had the same bottlenecked intensity behind their eyes as gamblers, but the energy was moving in the opposite direction—not outward, toward some romantic dream or delusion that convinces people to waste their lives in the hopes of leaving it all behind. It doesn't work this way for chess. Chess is vaccinated against players' delusions of self-worth. However special you think you are, enter the game's competitive circuits and your rating is held up for all to see and recalibrated accordingly after each game. "On the chessboard," Emanuel Lasker once observed, "lies and hypocrisy do not survive long." Both you and your opponents always know where you stand at any given moment. You can't bluff your way against eagerly duped, impatient opponents buying into wildly misguided notions of their own abilities.

There are exceptions, of course. Like the hustlers in Washington Square Park, just a few subway stops north of the Fulton Market. On my first visit to New York, in 2002, that was the first place I went, to the southwest corner of the park to see the Chess Plaza. By then it was no longer the living mecca of American chess where Stanley Kubrick and Bobby Fischer might have possibly faced off but rather a kind of open-air, sideshow-tent photo op for tourists. What costumed superheroes and cartoon characters were to Times Square, chess hustlers were to Washington Square Park. That afternoon all eighteen tables were occupied with a Dickensian ragtag crew of hustlers, mostly African American, their worn chess pieces and battered clocks neatly lined up, searchlight eyes casting around for victims.

There wasn't much action that afternoon. You could clearly hear the aching strains of a violin being played underneath the arch across the park. Most of the hustlers sat reading discarded newspapers or magazines. Others smoked cigarettes. Some ate sandwiches and picked off the crusts to flick away and feed the pigeons.

Then a tourist pair, husband and wife, approached, and suddenly the place sprang to life. The woman asked a hustler if her husband could sit at the board and pose with him for a photograph and was shocked to discover the chess player wanted five bucks. The wife countered with an offer of two. A hustler shouted at the husband in a gravelly voice, "You look like a chess player. Have a little respect for what we do and si'down to play for five. She can take your photo while you play. I'll spot you a knight. Two-minute game?"

"How about you have two minutes, I get five?" the husband said with a sly smirk.

"Hustling the hustler, huh? Let's play, champ."

The husband sat down. To all eyes but his, the hustler turned the game into a termite infestation, and with only two kings remaining on the board, the tourist had a draw. The hustler feigned incredulity and embarrassment, and that hooked the husband through the cheek snugly. Smiles curled on the lips of players at other tables. Even the husband's wife looked aroused, presumably for the first time in years.

"Double or nothing?" the hustler asked.

"Well . . . honey?" asked the husband.

The wife nodded. "One more."

The husband narrowly lost on time.

"Double or nothing again, champ?"

The wife was on to the scam finally and fiercely pulled her husband's sleeve.

"I better go," the husband said, then turned to his wife to placate her with a tilt of his head.

"So just *one* more," the hustler said. Stifled snickers across the plaza.

In the end, the husband was dragged away from the table after losing $80 at the board.

"Enjoy that photo, miss!" came the chorus.

But not here inside the Fulton Market. Nothing was rigged. Nothing was up anybody's sleeve. It was absent the crushing emptiness of watching gamblers' emotional lives wrung by a dealer's shuffle, or row after row of slot machine levers being pulled like oars on some hopeless slave ship by wretches pining for deliverance with the ever fading shore of a one-in-a-million jackpot. This room wasn't flooded with $O_2$ or chain-smoking old ladies with oxygen tanks. We weren't being carpet-bombed with Dean Martin jingles as on any garden-variety casino floor. And the most important difference: here nobody was yearning for Lady Luck's fairy dust. There were no house odds to worry about or ignore. Lies and hypocrisy are the crucial ingredients casinos use to exploit their customers. No-limit poker only speaks to the money involved; everything else shrivels into monotonous routine except the rich bloom of deception.

Not here. Chess offers the other extreme of the same theater—people manically driven by a quest toward the truth—yet exploits it equally.

In chess, everything is earned. And yet *nothing* is earned. There is no real profit. Before Bobby Fischer played for a quarter-million dollars in Iceland in 1972—more money than the highest-paid American football or baseball stars saw for an entire *season* of work at that time—the reigning world champion, Boris Spassky, had earned only $1,400 for his title at the previous championship. And while Magnus and Sergey were playing for $1.1 million, by far the biggest purse in chess, anyone outside the top thirty in chess had an easier time making a living selling arts and crafts or busking with an electronic piano on the subway than playing chess. At the 2017 US Chess Championship, the prize money offered to the winner was $50,000, while the bottom finisher among twelve players earned $4,000 (less than one-third of the annual US poverty line for an individual).

"It has all the beauty of art—and much more. It cannot be commercialized. Chess is much purer than art in its social position." So said the artist Marcel Duchamp, who at around the age of thirty pretty much abandoned his career for the game. "Nothing interests me more than to find the right move," he declared. Even after fifteen hundred years and successfully infecting a tenth of the world's population with its narcotic potency, was chess any closer to selling out even if it wanted to? If so, Vegas would have already done it. Vegas could and invariably *would* take anything that people couldn't resist and turn it for a buck. But not chess. Its metaphor—too *powerful*? too *weak*? too *ambiguous*?—couldn't be contaminated or pimped out like a poker chip.

All the feeble and clumsy attempts the championship organizers had made to transform chess into a more profitable enterprise only underlined how resolutely the game could never be anything but itself.

The Nordic grandmaster from the previous day was back again, continuing to awkwardly make the rounds, tirelessly gathering contact information, looking for the mother lode. I periodically checked in on Magnus and Sergey, but after just a few moves several people in the VIP lounge had groaned and predicted—correctly, it would turn out—another bloodless draw. Objectively it's true that four moves of a chess game offer over seventy thousand possible positions, and let both players have another move each and you're suddenly at nine million, and then we're up to 318 billion possible positions if you allow *another* move to each player. But that's how good these two guys were. They were able to see everything.

I ordered an orange juice from the bar and sat down at a vacant chessboard to watch Carlsen and Karjakin's progress. Just then an enormous Cheshire cat smile sat down at my table attached to a lovely African American woman with braids hanging down her shoulders, covered in black-and-white patterned clothes with a matching chessboard charm dangling from her neck. She held up a white pawn over the board.

"Would you like to play?" she asked in a cajoling tone. "I'm Adia."

Adia Onyango had introduced and taught chess to thousands of adults and kids for the past eleven years. While pursuing her doctorate in child clinical psychology, she had fought her way into the top one hundred of women's chess, where she's remained for four years. She organized tournaments and developed programs for other chess instructors. Her best friend taught her chess in junior high school, but it didn't take over her life until she was introduced to tournaments when she was an adult.

We talked for a while. My Washington Square Park story was on my mind. So was a YouTube video I'd seen of Magnus in the park, schooling a couple hustlers who had no clue who he was. I told Adia I wanted to find out who might be the most interesting street chess player in the country and then track them down.

"*Besides* Falafel Backgammon?" she asked, matter-of-factly pinning my rook in front of my king with her bishop.

"What's a Falafel Backgammon?" I asked.

"Not what, *who*. Falafel Backgammon is the nickname for Matvey Natanzon. He used to play in Washington Square Park while he was homeless. A lot of days he wouldn't earn enough money to buy anything but falafel sandwiches. That's how he got his name. Now he's the top-rated backgammon player in the world. He makes tens of thousands of dollars in less than an hour sometimes."

"Please, God, tell me you have some idea where I can find him," I said, tipping over my king in defeat.

"He moves around a lot. Israel. Las Vegas. Atlantic City. He's a compulsive gambler. I met Falafel at Bryant Park a few years ago. He grew up in Buffalo and I went to graduate school there and we knew some people from the chess scene in common there and here in New York. I can try and put you in touch with him."

Over the next four hours at Fulton Market, as Magnus and Sergey ground their way to another draw, I asked everyone I could about Falafel Backgammon, wondering if they knew how to track him down. Someone said he was in Los Angeles. Others said Israel or Las Vegas or touring Europe, gambling on anything and everything in his spare time. The myth of Falafel got stranger and more outlandish with each person I spoke with.

I spent all night trying to find his contact information online and calling acquaintances. I also read a profile of him *The New*

*Yorker* published a few years ago. I was interested in his story. But even more so, I wanted to know if he had any thoughts on Magnus. Finally I reached him in Vegas.

"It was an interesting time in my life," Falafel said with a laugh. He had a gruff, nasal voice. "I was homeless. I was trying to survive in New York from the chessboard and not having much luck. It was possible to survive hustling chess then. Now it would *never* be possible to do that, like it was before. Different times."

Falafel, né Matvey Natanzon, was born in Soviet Russia in 1969 and fled with only his mother to Israel, settling in the town of Azor, just outside Tel Aviv. Natazon's mother, Larissa, supported the family by working tirelessly at the airport for the next eleven years. When Natanzon was fourteen, his mother married an Israeli-American biophysicist Holocaust survivor and brought her teenage son to live with them in Buffalo. Natanzon had been comfortable with his mother in Azor and despised everything about Buffalo and his new disciplinarian stepfather. Matvey became known as Mike and simultaneously took his first stab at English *and* chess translating from chess books in Hebrew his stepfather had bought him. Natanzon began to drink and gamble. He was bullied by his parents to study accounting and business administration at the New York State University at Buffalo but proved a remarkably indifferent student. Gambling took over most of his attention.

After graduation he was adamantly against finding a job, and his increasing obsession with gambling on sports left him penniless. His parents refused to support him.

"My mother had kicked me out of the house," he said. "I

didn't have a job. I couldn't afford to live anywhere. No friends. No money. Nothing. I didn't have any skills. But I could play a little chess. In New York City there were always going to be tourists willing to play for a few bucks."

When he found out a friend was driving to Manhattan in the winter of 1994, Natanzon, who was then twenty-five, jumped in the car for the icy four-hundred-mile drive. Beyond some winter clothes, all Natanzon brought with him for luggage was a chessboard and a clock crammed inside a backpack.

"It was just like in the movies," he said. "Madonna showed up in New York broke too, maybe fifty dollars in her pocket."

He was determined to seek his fate and fortune on the tables at Chess Plaza inside Washington Square Park.

"*Searching for Bobby Fischer* had just come out in 1993. I arrived right after that. A chess movie gave a little buzz, but the scene in the park had been established a long time before that. It was really the end of an era that I walked into. All kinds of people were there then. If you want to call it chess hustling or whatever it was."

It was an inauspicious start. Instead of making money hand over fist on the park's famous chess tables as he dreamed, Natanzon ended up broke and sleeping under them.

"I just didn't like working," he said. "Sleeping in the park was better than going to work in a cubicle. I slept in the park. I slept in the subway. I slept wherever I could. When you've got nowhere to sleep it's a nightmare. It wasn't something I was used to. I wasn't used to eating falafels off street vendors all day either."

What money he did earn at the tables proved as easily stolen by pickpockets as lost against visiting grandmasters or stronger players. Then one morning as he slept under a chess table,

Natanzon's earsplitting snoring alerted one of the longtime players at the Chess Plaza, Russian Paul. For two dollars, Russian Paul hired Natanzon to guard and hold his favorite table every morning before he arrived. That money, the only steady income Natanzon enjoyed after struggling to earn anything hustling chess, invariably was spent on falafels from nearby restaurants. Before long Natanzon was known at the Chess Plaza only as Falafel. The local hustlers helped him with his game, but if he earned $25 for a day's work it was a good day. Falafel saw other men in the park earning a more comfortable living playing backgammon. Falafel bore into backgammon with fiendish intensity. He vowed to Russian Paul that one day he would be the best player in the world. But he did nothing but lose money. He remained homeless for the next six months.

When friends found Falafel a room, the monthly rent threatened to send him back down to the streets. In the meantime, the man who refused to dedicate himself seriously to anything throughout his life suddenly devoted nearly every waking hour to playing online backgammon in his room. "What was the money you could earn hustling tourists with chess?" I asked.

As his weight ballooned to over three hundred pounds, his dominance at backgammon gained him a considerable reputation. He was one of the early players to use a computer to accelerate his learning exponentially. Then, finally, he found some wealthy fish in New York to play and made real money fleecing them. Sometimes he could earn $100,000 in one good night playing backgammon. The boy who refused to find a real job had found his life's calling in a pair of dice.

"My relationship with backgammon is the exact opposite of

my personality everywhere else in my life," he said. "I'm very, very lazy. But when something captures my attention and I want to seek out the truth, I can *never* let go of it. I can't stop going at it. I think it might be something similar with Magnus Carlsen in chess today. Both of us got to become the best in the world in what we do for similar reasons, I think. He was a perfect fit for chess in exactly the same way I'm a perfect fit for backgammon. I was one of the better players at the park as a hustler, but if a GM or a very strong player showed up, I lost."

"You see something of yourself in Magnus?" I asked.

"I think we're similar, although I'm sure he's a lot more intelligent than I am." Falafel laughed. "He was obsessed with chess at an early age and it was all that mattered. Everything else was all out the window. He was focused and excelled to become the best in the world, *also* by way of computers. He was able to train with the help of computers, and I did the same thing in backgammon. They weren't available to players in chess or backgammon before to train with until very recently.

"In chess I wasn't able to rise above a certain level. Maybe I started too late. All the top players in chess start very early in their childhood. Like Magnus. In backgammon it's approached very differently. It's approached more like gambling, with kids discouraged because of the money. So most of us don't learn the game until later, when we're adults. So it was more of a level playing field when I took to it. I learned the game at twenty-five. The playing field was much different than chess. You can't make up that lost time."

"And in 2007 you lived up to your prophecy of becoming the top-rated player in the world," I said.

"Yes," he said, clearing his throat. "But if I hadn't found this, I don't know what would have happened to me."

"What if you'd stayed with chess?" I asked.

"That would have been impossible for me. I couldn't have survived. I've never had a real job in my life. People who play chess, the seriousness is very different."

"Do you see what you do with backgammon as an art or gambling?" I asked.

"I asked a rabbi about Judaism's attitude toward gambling. He said it was permitted but not as a means of making a living. Gambling makes you a parasite on society. What it all comes down to in the end is who wins and who loses. Every man plays out his luck. That's the truth of it. Everyone plays out his luck. I don't think this is how Magnus looks at his path."

# 6

# "WHY CAN'T HE
# BEAT THIS GUY?"

In 1822, only two miles north of the Fulton Market, where New York's Twenty-Sixth Street meets the East River, Bellevue Penitentiary was one of the first prisons in the country to adopt a new invention then getting rave reviews from England's prisons: the treadmill. New Yorkers were encouraged not just to watch but to *heckle* the thirty-two convicts causing a barrel-like machine to rotate via twelve hours' worth of soul-crushing, mind-numbing exertion. The convicts would grind dozens of unseen bushels of corn, which fed other inmates. Politicians loved the results, boasting that inmates subjected to this torture were so physically and emotionally defeated they could hardly utter a word. The governor of Massachusetts witnessed the effects and described the atmosphere as "orderly and submissive," adding that when the treadmill was combined with solitary confinement, the two punishments "furnish the most salutary punishment and the most powerful detriment from crime that the lenient spirit of our laws admits." One report, written by a physician tasked with assessing the effects of the treadmill on inmates, concluded that it was highly effective as a mode of punishment given how it was "peculiarly irksome; requiring a severe exertion of the body, but furnishing no employment of the mind." A rare scathing criticism arrived in the *Baltimore Patriot* republished from the *Edinburgh Review*'s evaluation of treadmills used in a northern England jail (here "irksome" is used to indict rather than praise the treadmill's efficacy in breaking down inmates): "The labor of the tread-mill is irksome, dull, monotonous, and disgusting to the last degree. A man does not see his work, does not know what he is making; there is no room for art, contrivance, ingenuity and superior skill—all which are the cheering substances of human labor."

Nearly a century later, on July 7, 1912, outside the Fulton Market's window, the East River flowing under the Brooklyn Bridge provided Harry Houdini a stage for one of his most famous escapes. Police had expressly forbidden him to use the pier for the dangerous stunt, which led Houdini to hire a tugboat with media and anxious spectators accompanying him onboard. Houdini was shackled in handcuffs and leg irons, wrapped in chains, placed inside a crate weighed down with two hundred pounds of lead, nailed in, and tossed overboard into the river. Two and a half minutes later, Houdini broke the surface of the water 250 feet away from where he had been dropped. The box was pulled back into the boat, where the detritus of Houdini's discarded chains and manacles lay sullenly in a heap.

The next five games between Magnus and Sergey offered something in between the previous two centuries' outlandish and punishing entertainments.

In game three, on the thirtieth move, Karjakin, playing with black pieces, took as long as twenty-five minutes to make one move during the game. The clock became a major factor in the game for him, and he dropped his rook well into Magnus's enemy territory and sent every chess beat reporter from Norway and Russia into a frenzy. Carlsen, for the first time in the match, had his opportunity for blood. Hours tensely hobbled by as he tried to seize his advantage and bring the game home. Over the course of the next forty moves, Karjakin fought with everything he had to not give another inch, but Magnus held his advantage going into the sixth hour of play. He was closing in for the kill just before his seventy-second move of the game. But instead he blundered. At this point in the game Carlsen possessed more powerful pieces than Karjakin, with an extra knight on the board. After Carlsen moved his rook to intimidate one of Karjakin's pawns, several spectators consulting the chess apps on their phones groaned in concert. "How could he not move his rook to put black's king in check!" one teenager scoffed. "He blew it!" Carlsen's narrow advantage erased, Karjakin engineered what was hailed in FIDE's official newsletter and several media outlets as a "draw for the ages." After Carlsen had methodically fastened Karjakin in a straitjacket of a position, pulling every strap to tighten its strangling grip, Karjakin dazzled the chess world by breaking free.

"Unbelievable game," said Judit Polgár from the commentators' booth as Karjakin made the final move of the game. "They are finishing nearly *seven hours* of play. Unbelievable roller-coaster game."

Carlsen looked up from the board in a daze and offered his hand. Applause broke out all over the venue in celebration of Karjakin's audacious escape. When both players arrived at the press conference, Karjakin was given a standing ovation. He smiled bashfully, looking like Hergé's Tintin after a perilous adventure safely navigated. Carlsen, weary of the room, his face drawn and skin pale, sat at the dais and moped sullenly.

The following day, in their fourth game, Carlsen and Karjakin sat down for another marathon. Six hours. Ninety-four moves. Carlsen stalked his opponent, looking to exploit a limited material advantage, while Karjakin's strategy seemed to be something akin to building a sandcastle to dam an incoming tide. It became apparent the previous game had taken its toll on Carlsen when, after the seventeenth move, he stood up from the board and retreated to the private players' room to sprawl out over a couch with his hands covering his weary eyes. When Carlsen discovered that cameras in the private room offered this vulnerable spectacle to hundreds of thousands of his fellow countrymen in Norway, staying up till ungodly hours to watch their national hero online, he successfully petitioned to have the private players' room barred from camera view. It got no easier for Carlsen, however. Midway through the game, on the forty-fifth move, Carlsen again let his advantage slip between his fingers. Karjakin's sandcastle had become an impenetrable fortress capable of withstanding the siege.

By the fifth game, seeing the effects of four draws on Carlsen's bearing and demeanor, spectators at the Fulton Market began to murmur about faint echoes of 1984's brutal world championship between Kasparov and Karpov that the guy on the escalator had told me about the first day. Sergey Karjakin, despite playing with black pieces (always one step behind), for the first time in the championship poured on the pressure and took control of the board during a hopelessly complex middle game. After four games of playing the careful counterpuncher to Carlsen's aggressions on the board, Karjakin, with a narrow advantage after the Giuoco Piano (Quiet Game) opening, was obliged to lead the dance. Carlsen was suddenly in danger of falling behind in a world championship for the first time in his life. There were gasps from the chess media and visiting grandmasters by 6 p.m. when, with Carlsen's forty-first move, he made his biggest blunder of the match. Nobody could know what was in Carlsen's mind as he retreated his king to g2 behind pawn on the h-file. Potentially he saw the game as yet another draw he wished to accelerate, but every grandmaster, chess mind, and laptop wielder around me clearly recognized the superior move would have been sliding his rook over to the edge of the board to position himself for a late-game attack. Carlsen's king had roadblocked that strategy and any hope of siccing his rook on Karjakin's king. Unwittingly, Carlsen had flipped the keys of his kingdom over to Karjakin.

Unfortunately for Karjakin, he was unable to exploit it. After five hours and fifty-one moves, both men shook hands for another draw. At the postgame press conference, I noticed that while Karjakin's stammer had diminished with each ensuing draw, Carlsen's unease, tics, and impatience were growing more apparent. He readily acknowledged his forty-first was an unmitigated disaster. "King to g2 is a huge blunder," Carlsen conceded with agitation, dejectedly cradling his jaw in the palm of his hand.

The sixth game felt like watching two prizefighters take a round off and have a breather. After just thirty-two moves and not even two hours, an uneventful draw was agreed to. For the first time, the November sky outside the Fulton Market wasn't dark when the game ended. But the result was the same: another draw.

At the postgame press conference, an adorable boy no older than six, wearing a sweater and oversize glasses, grabbed a microphone and confronted both players: "When are you expecting your first win?"

As the crowd roared approval, both players smiled. It was the first time since the championship began that both men looked to be having any fun *at the same time*.

The players had the next day off, then returned on Sunday to the Fulton Market for game seven. It was a bitter winter morning. The temperature was hovering around freezing. The world championship match had been getting shine. The *New York Times* had already written five articles about it. According to press reports from Scandinavia, upward of 7 percent of the entire population of Norway were staying up until the wee hours to watch Carlsen during the games. Over in Germany, *Die Zeit*'s chess coverage was being read more than anything else in their sports section. A shivering sellout crowd of spectators lined up outside the venue. It was only the second game played on a weekend, and hordes of kids from across New York City's five boroughs—and many others who had flown in with their parents from across the country—gathered impatiently in the South Street Seaport plaza, eagerly waiting for the doors to open. Several kids I saw waiting outside, their parents nearby holding chessboards under their arms, could barely keep still for asking about Magnus Carlsen and if they might see him finally get on the scoreboard.

"Why can't he beat this guy?" one little boy asked his dad.

His dad shrugged. "I'm sure Magnus is asking himself that same question right now."

And so was the chess world.

Inside the venue, another father and son were sitting across from one another at the chessboard in the VIP room: famed astrophysicist Neil deGrasse Tyson and his teenage son, Travis. Tyson wore cowboy boots. His son had a medicine ball–size Afro.

I barged in on them to ask Tyson what brought him to the game.

"My son took a very serious interest in chess and there's the great measure, 'How old is your kid when they first beat you, the parent?' That happened very early with Travis, when he was like *nine* or something."

As Tyson's wonderful deep laugh poured out across the room, his son paid no attention, instead studying his position on the board.

"He *started* beating me, and then the rate at which he beat me became more and more reliable, more and more predictable. We reached the point where he was beating me twenty-nine games out of thirty. That's when he started joining the chess club and entering tournaments. And only then, at the chess tournament, they were selling chess swag and one of the things they were offering was a book called *How to Beat Your Dad at Chess*. But he was already doing that, so we didn't have to buy it."

Judging by Travis's shy smirk, he had clearly heard this anecdote told before.

"There are enough people who value being good at something mental that chess is no longer a shunned, nerdy thing. The richest guy in the world is a patron saint of nerds, Bill Gates, so these times are different from decades ago when that was not the case. I attended the tournaments and it was always fun to see who won and who didn't. Who could lose and be emotionally stable about it. You know kids have a lot invested. If that's what you're good at and you think you're good and your parents think you're good and they put you up at every next tournament level it gets harder and harder. At some point you run into a person that blows you away and you have to look in the mirror and say, 'Am I done, or do I keep going to try to be better?'

"I think everyone needs to encounter that in some category of their life, at some time in their life, and for many of the kids it can happen on the chessboard. Of course a lot of us got interested in the chess movies. *Searching for Bobby Fischer* and, just recently, *Pawn Sacrifice*. I was so disappointed to see how poorly both did at the box office. They both lost money."

"What do you make of the fact that six hundred million people play this game and only the slightest fraction of the top one percent can make a living at it?" I asked. "Many grandmasters told me only about thirty players in the world can survive *just* playing chess."

"It doesn't have the financial depth that most other things we celebrate do. And that's a curious fact. I don't know, does it need better marketing? Do the singularly great players need to be weirder in their personality? Did Bobby Fischer need his weirdness to drive an audience? Or it could also maybe have something to do with the fact that it's played here in a back room in seclusion in a soundproof booth. I mean, does chess take more concentration than a baseball player in the bottom of the ninth with the bases loaded, game seven of the World Series? The fans are screaming and there's a ball coming at you at ninety-five miles an hour and you have a round stick to hit it with. No one is saying, 'Let's be silent.' I compare that with golf, where, imagine you're a baseball player and you didn't know anything of golf and someone is describing it to you. You say, 'They want silence on a golf course? How fast is the ball moving?' Not at all. 'Where is it?' It's sitting at their feet. 'What are they hitting it with? Something much smaller than the ball?' No, something much bigger than the ball. That must just be so odd. But I don't know with chess. I don't have the silver bullet here.'

Tyson stared blankly for a moment.

"Here is something I have not resolved in my own thought," he said. "I don't know any single other thing that all great chess players are also good at. Chess may be singular and unique as its own game. If you're good at Monopoly, that can help you negotiate a real estate deal. If you're good at poker, it can help you bluff. Okay. Poker people make good bluffers in conversation. I don't know what other one thing all chess players are good at, other than being good at chess. I've thought about it. I don't have a clear sense of what Magnus Carlsen, as brilliant as he is on the chessboard, could be doing somewhere else."

A commotion caught Tyson's eye at a table nearby, which was concealed by two layers of fixed humanity encircling the board. We both went over to investigate and discovered the inner layer was comprised of children, behind whom were equally enchanted adults. In the center of the vortex was twenty-four-year-old Brooklyn-born Fabiano Caruana, the second-highest-rated player in the world—his hands blurring as mystifyingly as those of any elite prizefighter as he tried to finish off his opponent at blitz chess.

There is something of a hummingbird quality to Caruana's physical presence that gives one a vague suspicion he might be the illegitimate love child of Malcolm Gladwell. It was strange to see him there. Had he not lost to Sergey in the Candidates Tournament, it would have been him sitting across from Magnus in the executioner's room. And yet he'd shown up anyway. And he was playing strangers. It was as if Rafael Nadal had lost a US Open semifinal match yet showed up on Championship Sunday to play on the Arthur Ashe Stadium side courts against ticketholders. You would never see this in any other sport. Which of course led to the eternal question: Was chess a sport or was it an art, a science, or, most tantalizingly of all, some kind of Bermuda Triangle of human intellect? Whatever you called it, seeing Caruana there—not simply watching or networking but *playing*—was further proof of just how unrelentingly addictive the damn game was.

After Caruana dispensed with his opponent he looked over at one of the flat-screens hanging in the VIP room to monitor the progress.

"Draw," he said flatly.

And he would be right. Game seven was on its way to an uninspired stalemate after thirty-three moves and two and a half hours at the board.

"Another game?" his opponent asked.

Caruana nodded absentmindedly. He set up his pieces and went to slap the clock but stopped his hand in midair. A little boy leaned in too close to watch. His nose was in the way. The little boy's big brother, maybe nine, yanked him back by the collar. Caruana smiled and slapped the clock, and another game began.

# 7

# A PLACE THAT
# TIME FORGOT

During the championship off days, I'd been spending time in the New York Public Library's rare-books section. I kept thinking of those tables in Washington Square Park. And not just those tables but the tables at parks all over the city: Union Square, Bryant Park, Columbus Park, Central Park's Chess & Checkers House, Marcus Garvey Park in Harlem, City Hall Park downtown, Tompkins Square Park, even the scattered tables on islands dividing Broadway up in Hamilton Heights. How had New York and chess become so intertwined?

The best that I could determine, the story begins in the mid-nineteenth century with Paul Morphy. Morphy was born into wealth and was already a spooky child prodigy by the age of nine, beating almost any adult in New Orleans. In 1849, by the time he was twelve, he was even crushing visiting masters like Hungary's Johann Löwenthal at the board. After receiving his law degree at age twenty, still too young to legally practice law, Morphy focused his attention back on chess and accepted an invitation from the First American Chess Congress to come to New York. There, he ended up becoming the United States' first chess champion.

The following year Morphy traveled across Europe and toured royal courts and prestigious social gatherings, whereupon he destroyed nearly every challenger effortlessly. The American media eagerly grabbed onto the story—setting off what came to be described as "Morphy Mania"—and the popularity of the game soared on local soil. Chess clubs opened up everywhere from Philadelphia to St. Louis but especially in Manhattan and Brooklyn. *The Book of the First American Chess Congress* was published in 1857 by Daniel Willard Fiske, who dedicated the book to Paul Morphy, inscribing below his name, "The hero of that American tournament whose story is here told, and the conqueror upon the traditional battle fields of Europe, I dedicate this book with every sentiment of esteem and friendship." By 1857, several American cities were vying for the right to hold the first American Chess Congress. Philadelphia laid claim, with Ben Franklin having played the first game of chess ever recorded on the continent there nearly 125 years before (we know he played from at least 1733). The first chess book published in America, in 1802, came from a Philadelphia press. Chicago had the most organized and largest chess club in the country. Washington was the federal capital and the easiest place in which to gather amateurs from the South. Baltimore, Cincinnati, and New Orleans threw their hats into the ring. Finally, after a great deal of jockeying for position, "other cities peacefully and courteously yielded to the earnestly urged claims of New York, and it was finally determined that the first American Chess Congress should convene in that city, on the sixth day of October, 1857."

Three decades later, the city also hosted the very first official World Chess Championships—the title for which Magnus and Sergey would eventually vie. This was in 1886, back when the American flag had only thirty-eight stars and the torch on the not-yet-green Statue of Liberty had only been lit six months earlier, the year in which Ty Cobb would be born and Emily Dickinson would die. Wilhelm Steinitz of Austria and Johannes Zukertort of Poland played in New York's Cartier's Hall on Fifth Avenue (the New School stands on the location today). The tidy sum of four grand (equivalent to just under $100,000 in today's purchasing power) was on the line, but Steinitz was even more interested in the prize of remaining in America. The youngest of a tailor's thirteen sons to survive, Steinitz had been born in a Jewish ghetto of Prague in 1836. He learned the game at twelve and grew increasingly obsessed with chess in his twenties after moving to Vienna to study math at university. He became one of the top players of the nineteenth century. Hoping to escape rising anti-Semitism back home, he changed his name from Wilhelm to William, insisted on playing next to an American flag, and encouraged the press to bill him as being "of New York." He would win, and two years later he became an American citizen.

The Manhattan Chess Club was founded in 1877 with a membership of thirty-six players. Membership dues were $4 a year. Women weren't allowed to join as members until 1938, sixty-one years later. The club hosted its first tournament in 1878, and four years later, world champion William Steinitz became a member. The Manhattan Chess Club hosted two of Steinitz's world championship wins, in 1886 and 1889. The club again hosted eight games of a world championship in 1894, when Emmanuel Lasker dethroned Steinitz on his way to remaining champion for the next twenty-seven years. Lasker became a member shortly after his victory. Legendary Cuban champion José Capablanca joined in 1909 (and would die from a stroke inside the club while watching a game in 1942). Bobby Fischer joined fourteen years after Capablanca's death.

The Marshall Chess Club arrived in 1915, located at 70 West Thirty-Sixth Street, formed with a handful of players led by Frank Marshall, US chess champion (he held that title from 1909 to 1936 and was one of the game's original five grandmasters). Marshall once competed for a world title, in 1907, but was routed 8–0 by Lasker. The club moved around the city until members put together enough money to buy a clubhouse in Greenwich Village in 1922. Membership became a status symbol in New York, with the board of governors including such major names in business and society as Edward Cornell, Gilbert Colgate, Henry Leeds, and George Emlen Roosevelt. Since 1931, the club has resided at 23 West Tenth Street in a two-story brownstone built in 1832, purchased with the help of wealthy patrons. Marshall and his wife lived in the club and looked after it until his death in 1944, with his widow taking over leadership until her death in 1967. Huge sports figures like golfer Bobby Jones could be seen playing one day, famous artists like Marcel Duchamp the next. Capablanca's favorite chess table is still given pride of place in the club, residing in the rear drawing room. Stanley Kubrick joined in the early 1950s and routinely offered to pay his dues "from my winnings." Bobby

Fischer arrived as a moody thirteen-year-old and on October 17, 1956, electrified the chess world with his "Game of the Century" against twenty-six-year-old Donald Byrne. Nine years later, when the US Department of State refused to issue Fischer a visa to play in Cuba in the Capablanca Memorial tournament, Fischer competed from Capablanca's favorite table in the Marshall's rear drawing room, wiring moves to Havana via teletype.

These two institutions, the Marshall and the Manhattan Chess Clubs, were the pillars of chess in America. In the 1930s, rampant anti-Semitism led to a huge influx of Jewish intellectuals in New York, many of whom brought their chess addiction with them. The Great Depression also increased the popularity of chess, as many people were desperate for any means of scraping together money. Bronx-born Arnold Denker, who would go on to become a United States champion, hustled chess during the Depression all over the city. Before Humphrey Bogart could make a living as an actor on Broadway and later in film, he made ends meet with a chessboard and a clock hustling speed chess (it was Bogart who inserted in the script that viewers of *Casablanca* first meet Rick Blaine at the chessboard). Al Horowitz, who would become the first chess columnist for the *New York Times*, hustled right along with them. Soon enough, New York became to chess what Paris had been to art. The late 1940s was when many picnic tables in Washington Square Park were converted to chess tables.

In 1952, Russian-born Nicolas Rossolimo emigrated with his family to New York City from France. Rossolimo was a formidable chess player who'd won the French championship in 1948 and finished second to world champion José Raúl Capablanca in a

Paris tournament ten years earlier. A year after arriving in the US, Rossolimo earned his grandmaster title, yet learned all too quickly that even grandmasters could never hope to make a living. He would declare, "America, I decided, is a better country for my wife, a better country for my son, a better country for everyone *but* chess players." He took menial work as a busboy at the Waldorf Astoria, waited tables at restaurants, folded clothes at a Laundromat, played the accordion, and drove taxis while adopting the Manhattan Chess Club as a second home. According to legend, Bobby Fischer sat down as a boy to play Rossolimo and was left in tears. Three years after arriving in New York, Rossolimo won the 1955 US Open Chess Championship.

In 1958, Rossolimo invested his life savings to open a chess studio in Greenwich Village, where the likes of Duchamp, Jack Kerouac, John Coltrane, and William S. Burroughs popped in for games. To scrape together the rent money, he played tournaments, continued to drive a cab, sold chess sets, taught lessons, and charged guests for simultaneous chess exhibitions. Fischer and Duchamp were regulars.

In 1972, with the Fischer boom in full effect across America, Rossolimo was playing a tournament in Spain. While he was away, George Frohlinde, whom Rossolimo had hired to run the day-to-day operations of the chess studio for several years, according to Rossolimo let the studio fall apart. When Rossolimo returned, the two fought over the business until it closed down. Frohlinde quickly opened a new studio on Thompson Street. Rossolimo sought revenge, opening a *new* studio across the street from Frohlinde's Village Chess Shop. The two never spoke again. Rossolimo, one of America's twelve living grandmasters, died under mysterious circumstances after falling down a flight of stairs while leaving a Greenwich Village apartment where he'd given a chess lesson in 1975. His shop closed shortly after.

Frohlinde got into another rivalry in 1995. One of his managers, Imad Khachan, claimed that Frohlinde had reneged on a promise to make him a partner. So he opened the Chess Forum across the street, where it exists to this day. Frohlinde's went under in 2012.

The same year the Chess Forum opened was also the last time prior to 2016 that the World Chess Championship was hosted in New York. Garry Kasparov and Viswanathan Anand sat across a chessboard on the 107th floor of the south tower of the World Trade Center on September 11, 1995. Exactly six years to the day later, on September 11, 2001, only a mile and a half south of the Chess Forum, the World Trade Center was attacked. By 10:28 that morning, both towers had fallen. Nearly three thousand people died, and over six thousand more were injured. The Chess Forum's owner, Imad Khachan, who lived next door to his shop, at 217 Thompson Street, was dragged out of bed to open the shop by players literally covered in debris from the collapsed towers.

"They needed to play," Khachan told me, and smiled inside his shop over a cup of steaming lemon tea. Chopin was playing quietly in the shop, a worn carpet was spread over the floor. "So many people were stranded in the city. There was nowhere for anyone to go that morning who had checked out of their hotels. No taxis. No planes. No subways. No hotels. Cars were restricted for fear of suicide attack. So many people roaming the city that day, dragging their luggage with nowhere to go. Everything was closed. We were open. They came here to sort out their next move. They came here to find a sanctuary from all the madness outside. The smell was here from the towers. For months you had that smell from the building and those thousands of burned people."

A man named Aaron Louis was in the shop with me and Khachan. He had also been a manager at the Village Chess Shop. He now works as the director of audiovisual at the Museum of Modern Art and as a freelance producer. Louis recalled that day: "I was on my way to the Chess Shop when the first plane hit the tower. My cousins were in the towers. So I went down there after they got out and I worked triage for thirty-six hours. When I got back to the chess shop, people were covered in dust and still playing. Everyone coming down the street was covered in dust and had to have somewhere to go. They never went home. Everyone they knew, their family was there. The owners recognized that and wouldn't close. Some people who were evacuated from the towers went to the Chess Shop and just kept playing. Never left. It was the only way they could deal with the trauma. After the attacks, we stayed open for days and kept the lights on."

The Chess Forum stayed open too.

"After a shift I'd go down to the World Trade Center and help search for survivors," Khachan said. "I volunteered at the distribution center. And then I'd come back here and do my best to look after the people in my shop."

Khachan grew up in war-torn Beirut with eight siblings and left Lebanon as a teenage refugee. He arrived in New York at age twenty-two in 1987. His parents were schoolteachers. Khachan attended New York University as a graduate student but dropped out just before finishing his PhD in comparative religion. He'd fallen in love, not so much with chess, but with chess *culture*. Which wasn't nearly as polite and refined as most outsiders might think.

"I came from Lebanon," Khachan said. "A civil war was tearing apart my country with unspeakable violence. But in all my years, I never felt as threatened in my life as working at Frohlinde's chess shop. I carried a knife to work. Many of the hustlers in Washington Square Park learned chess in prison. A lot of them dealt drugs. We didn't allow gambling but they'd come in anyway. Other times thieves, degenerates, fights at the board. The police were furious with us. They told us they would stop coming. One person from Bellevue Hospital escaped and the police chased him on horses when he came to the Village. He came here. The police horse was half inside the store as they chased him."

A mother walked into the shop and asked if her son could stay and play for an hour while she finished some shopping. Khachan went to make the kid some hot chocolate. Kids play for free at the shop. Everyone else has to pay a dollar an hour.

Aaron Louis offered to play a few games with the kid. "Miles Davis used to drop his son off for chess lessons the same way," he said. "Or just to have the chess players babysit. He'd play a set and come back. Yoko Ono came in all the time when I was working, bringing in Sean for lessons. Jacques Chirac would drop in totally unannounced and you'd see him in heated games with homeless people. Abbie Hoffman worked behind the counter."

Khachan gave the kid the hot chocolate and sat back down.

"How often do you play?" I asked him.

"I don't get high on my own supply," he said. "I have an addictive personality. I'm a diabetic and I can't stop eating sugar."

"Is chess more addictive than sugar?" I asked.

"*Much* more addictive. And much more dangerous. Worse

than cocaine or any drug. A man moved here from France—math background—with a wife and beautiful baby. He played checkers but discovered chess in the park. That's that. Wife takes baby and leaves him forever. He lives in a shelter now. Many who come here have stories like that. Many worse who play in the park. Another man was an expert in calligraphy—had had his work displayed in the Smithsonian—until he found chess and ended up living in the White House, what the homeless called the shelter on Bowery. Others live in the mission."

Louis overheard our conversation. "Chess is only good for itself," he said. "For kids as a learning tool, certainly it offers some help. But at a certain point it becomes an addiction that prevents you from doing anything else. That was true for me and most of the people I saw coming in. I saw countless people wasting their whole lives in that shop. Their whole lives! Physicists, professors, massive careers, money, families—they lost everything. Many ended up homeless, and chess became all they cared about. Chess feels like heavy conversation but it's not. You *feel* like you're interacting, but really you're totally disconnected. You're lost in that world when you're awake and then you dream about it when you're asleep. I did. I had to stop playing just to hang on to the rest of my life. I wasn't even especially good. I was nothing compared to most of the people who came into the shop."

"And there's no Chess Anonymous to treat it, like an NA or AA," Khachan said. "The loss and win from it. Revenge and euphoria. One drink can be too much, and the ocean not enough. No. I'm a warden in a prison. A bartender to alcoholics. A croupier in a casino. This is a culture of addiction where parents bring their children to get hooked, like drug dealers."

"Prisons make money in America," I said. "Bars make money. Casinos make money. How on earth can you make money?"

"The internet killed any hope of making it a business," Khachan said. "It's cost me ever having a wife. It's cost me ever having children and enjoying a family. But I made my choice and these people are my family. I borrow and do everything I can to look after them and survive. With the banking crisis, they bail out Wall Street. But nobody will bail me out for this. This place was never designed to take. It *gives*. It's a place that time forgot. My real payment is the children and their faces. This city is about hype. Do you see any hype here? No. There is something genuine here."

"So this isn't a business, it's a charity?" I asked.

"It's a social service. Community service. We are not called a store or a shop. It's a *forum*. A place for ideas, not for money. Discussion. I came from a war. Conflict here isn't about stepping outside to settle disputes. We come *inside*. We find a board. That's where we settle our differences. There are many ideas protected here—chess is just *one* of them. I have created a refuge. New York City is more similar to Dubai now than the place I arrived to many years ago. Marie Antoinette said, 'Let them eat cake.' Here the starving are offered smartphones in the same spirit. This city was always for the rich and the poor. But now you *feel* it so much more. But chess brought them together. It's so beautifully democratic that way."

"Has the city sold its soul?" I asked.

"How can we judge? We sold our souls to chess. You can't take the rewards to the bank with chess, but you do take them to the grave. Unless you are one of the top ten players, that's your only reward."

I asked him what he thought of Magnus.

Khachan shrugged.

"Magnus came into this shop at twenty and looked fourteen. He beat everybody and nobody knew who he was. Now we all know who he is but don't really care. Why do I say this? Nothing against him or his games. But because the championship priced out the chess community by design. It's a dollar an hour here. Coming from a war-torn city in Lebanon, in New York every step something is trying to take money from you continuously. What is free here? This is a last refuge, to save and protect some semblance of value beyond what is bought and sold. We invited Kasparov to come here once and he asked for thirty thousand dollars for a twenty-minute visit. The championship match was a money grab. If my people can't go, I don't go. When Kasparov played in 1995 at the World Trade Center, tickets were affordable. We went. No hype. There were real people who went to see Kasparov. Grandmasters and shabby people. Chess people. For chess. Whenever the *New York Times* wrote about Magnus at the championship they were more interested in the amenities inside the VIP section and politics, and chess was an afterthought. Fischer was an artist. Magnus's victories are like drone strikes."

# 8

# ON THE EDGE OF THE ABYSS

In the VIP lounge, Henrik Carlsen stood nervously staring at one of the flat-screens. After eleven days, 415 moves, and thirty-eight hours, his son was in trouble.

The eighth game had started off with Carlsen hurling himself recklessly toward a decisive outcome and going for broke after seven grueling draws in a row. Even though many critics had observed that the champion might not be displaying his top form since beginning the match in New York, for the first time you could palpably feel Carlsen asserting his will against Karjakin with the force of being the greatest player on earth. The trouble was, Karjakin responded to that challenge with more confidence than he had ever displayed. Playing as white, Carlsen came out swinging, yet advantage oscillated violently between the two players.

After developing his pieces behind an envoy of pawns in an opening called the Colle-Zukertort System, Magnus found that time increasingly became a precarious issue as early as the twenty-fifth move, and he only became emboldened as the game progressed. Even when a match was more or less equal, Carlsen stubbornly took risks to achieve a win when a draw was available. Both competitors in a championship match receive a hundred minutes to complete their first forty moves (receiving an additional thirty-second bonus with each move) and gain the lifeline of an additional fifty minutes only after their fortieth move. The freakish complexity on the board during the middle game only caused each player to dangerously devour more time in hopes of his position not collapsing like a house of cards. It felt like we were watching two young men dropped into the ocean struggling furiously to escape time's devious straitjacket and not drown.

Seven moves later, on the thirty-second, Carlsen was down to six minutes on his clock, while Karjakin had only five. Carlsen conspicuously avoided any available options to force a draw and instead transformed the complexion of the game into a mad scramble for survival. A Carlsen blunder two moves later tossed a gun over to Karjakin in their knife fight and handed him the most promising position of the match. The Russian improved his chances after rooks were traded and Karjakin dispensed with one of Carlsen's pawns. Carlsen was staring down at two black pawns with a clear path toward coronation as queens at the end of the board. But Karjakin had let his time run down to less than a minute before making a move and risked losing by the clock not once, but with *five* successive, heart-wrenching, "Cut the blue wire!" "*What blue wire? I'm fucking color-blind!*" *Mission: Impossible*-worthy ending moves in a row. Karjakin had all of *seven* seconds remaining on his clock when he placed his fortieth move.

All at once, both players could breathe again. Karjakin suddenly had time to reflect on a winning move he'd discovered and squandered only a few moves earlier without the time to puzzle through whether or not it worked. Carlsen quickly rebounded to threaten a very exposed, weak black king standing alone surrounded by empty squares near one corner of the board. Karjakin abandoned whatever strategy he'd had to attack and pulled his queen back to defend. Carlsen helped himself to a pawn (now up on material) and placed the black king in check with his queen. The Russian's queen moved over to stand between them as the last line of defense. Carlsen repeated this dance step sliding diagonally onto Karjakin's back row. Both players recalibrated for a few moves. After nearly five hours at the board, on the forty-ninth move, threatening a worthless pawn with his queen, Carlsen squandered yet another draw opportunity in the most decisive mistake of the game. How much was the pressure getting to him at that point?

I remembered what Carlsen's oldest sister had once said about her brother always climbing mountains. Henrik had been by his side for every step of the way as Magnus attempted to reach the summits of ever greater mountains. In 2013, when Magnus fought for his first world title against Viswanathan Anand, Henrik was as close as he could be to his son while commentators suggested that Magnus's quest was equal to "climbing Everest in tennis shoes with no oxygen."

But with Carlsen having experienced so many close calls this game, nearly losing to time and making shockingly uncharacteristic mistakes, my imagination went in the suffocating opposite direction from mountaintops as I tried to understand the pressure Carlsen might be under right then. Perhaps the *rapture of the deep* might be some kind of Rosetta stone into the journey Carlsen took with his art. The rapture of the deep is what deep-sea divers, having plunged to highly pressurized and dangerous depths, poetically refer to as the effects of nitrogen narcosis. In the vast, cold darkness of the ocean's deep waters, your heart struggles to beat at more than half its rate. The pressure builds until your eardrums are ready to burst. Your lungs squeeze terribly inside your chest. Sometimes divers not only forget the way back to the surface, they lose all inclination to return. What divers call "Martini's law" suggests that the impairment of your judgment is the equivalent of consuming a martini for each ten meters you sink below twenty. The narcosis seeps into your consciousness like a deviously complex potion and can offer immediate serenity, profound tranquility, and the feeling that you're totally in control of your environment in a way you've never been before. Then vertigo might set in. You're strapped into a roller coaster, feeling unbridled exhilaration one moment, debilitating anxiety and hopelessness the next. Unadulterated euphoria whiplashes into manic paranoia. Stay a little longer, continue a little deeper, and soon you might not be alone down there, hallucinations and auditory disturbances lurking all around you. And the longer you remain in this state, the more the risk of a potentially fatal encounter with the bends awaits your return to the surface. Your body has potentially irrevocably lost the ability to adapt to an atmosphere it's known all your life at the surface.

The endgame gave no clear advantage to either player after fifty moves had been played. Only one move later, all of Carlsen's options for survival were suddenly annulled. His demise was inevitable and I'd never seen a lonelier-looking human being in my life, trying to decide in what order to abandon his identity and his life. Karjakin calmly slid his pawn to a2 for his fifty-second move of the marathon battle and tapped his clock, scrawled the move's coordinates onto his score sheet, and leaned back in his goofy Staples chair. He exhaled and then allowed himself one sudden, momentous, life-defining, clandestine yet once-in-a-lifetime gratifying glance into Magnus's eyes to determine how the best-protected king in history felt having his throat slit. After taking his prize, Karjakin avoided looking directly into Carlsen's face and meandered over the board and around the room as he retreated into himself and relished the drawn-out suicide ritual to follow. If one could gain any purchase into what it meant in the dark mythos of chess supremacy, it was hands down one of the most cold-blooded, surreal, gloriously understated displays of sadistic delight I'd ever witnessed: chess's answer to Lee Harvey Oswald scrawling his name on the wall of history with the blood of JFK.

In the VIP lounge, people weren't watching the match. They were watching Henrik watch the match. It was Henrik upon whom Magnus had always bestowed the most credit for his phenomenal success. Yet Henrik had publicly confessed that he wasn't sure if his son could ever have been good at anything else. "I don't know what he could have become had he not played chess," he said in a 2013 interview. By the age of nine, Magnus could already easily beat his father at the chessboard and had little interest in doing anything else with his life besides play the game. Henrik's supportive and loving eyes had been following his son's progress on the board from the first day. Henrik had introduced the game to his son. Now, while Magnus struggled, his father couldn't tear himself away from his boy's face. His struggle reminded me of what Errol Morris and I had talked about: the terrible sacrificial calculation that sensational accomplishment and success require to arrive at their deliverance, and what a gross lie that is. How it's those *closest* to greatness—the unexceptional, the ordinary, the unsung and overlooked, those who barnacle themselves *to* the exceptional— who must sacrifice everything so that champions can abandon nearly all the ordinary responsibilities of life. Henrik's expression was naked and primal in its concern and completely prejudiced regarding everything he adored about his son. It was impossible to watch Henrik endure this outcome and not feel more sympathy for him than for his only son. Because as much as Magnus cared about chess—possibly to the point of risking the total self-destruction that he had hinted at—I had no doubt that his father cared even more about him.

I couldn't bear to watch Henrik anymore. I left the VIP lounge and went to stand in front of the window to the executioner's room.

"Carlsen is human after all," someone whispered.

"This is about to get very bloody," said someone else. "This wasn't supposed to happen to Magnus."

Behind the soundproof glass, Magnus looked like a boy terrorized by crippling fear, afraid both to look and not look under his bed for the monster that lurked beneath. But now that monster infected his imagination. There was no escape. How long was he willing to prolong the inevitable? He kept combing the board for possibilities while his body writhed in his jiggling chair. Discarding one hopeless avenue, he flicked his eyebrows. Then Carlsen compulsively began to blink until he began rubbing his eyes. For a split second, he almost sucked on his thumb before resting it against his chin.

As much as Carlsen relished his role of the most terrifying force in the world on a chessboard, as a boy he'd been ruthlessly terrorized by the gentle children of benevolent Norwegians because of his unique brilliance and unique eccentricity. Carlsen now offered an intimate corridor from which to view the fragile underbelly beneath the Sphinx-like nature of his genius and what fertilized it. As his time wore dangerously down, it was obvious, just this once, that his inability to let go of a defeated battlefield wasn't what made him a unique genius. Instead it laid bare the fragility and vulnerability of his universal humanity that tied all of us watching to him.

I had spent most of my adult life covering the red-light districts of sports, from prizefighting to bullfighting, and it had never occurred to me that the stakes involved regarding a chessboard could be just as high as those inside a boxing ring or the Plaza de Toros. Up close, this spectacle was no less disturbing. A young man in the prime of his life was mentally and emotionally imploding in slow motion, much to another's barely restrained delight.

Probably the closest Magnus had come to this kind of crushing defeat was twelve years before, at the FIDE World Chess Championship in Libya. Carlsen was thirteen and the youngest competitor ever to participate in an FIDE World Chess Championship. The tournament had been created with the intention of having the winner play Garry Kasparov, the world's top player, and represented a move toward a reunification of the World Chess Championship, which had been split into two separate titles since 1993. Carlsen lost to Levon Aronian in the opening round. As his time expired, he fell back in his chair and closed his eyes to avoid the nightmare confronting him. "My whole world fell apart," Carlsen told a documentary film crew in his shaky, boyish voice. He retreated to a dark hotel room, unable to sleep.

Confronted with the present situation, Magnus remained still, leaning over the table like an old ship's figurehead. Then dread and nerves set in, and even more tics and contortions sprouted about his face. His squirming got worse—he was almost in convulsions. I thought of the *60 Minutes* interview.

"But you enjoy it when you see your opponent squirm?" Bob Simon had asked.

"Yes, I *do*," Magnus had said. "I enjoy it when I see my opponent really suffering."

Even after only a handful of moves, the sixty-four squares of a chessboard can seem like an infinite desert far larger than the Sahara. In fact, there are far more possible chess moves than grains of sand in all the deserts of the world combined.

Now that horrifying excess spread out in all directions before Carlsen. The clock ticked down for one minute and forty-eight seconds after Karjakin made his last move. Silently Carlsen desperately searched for some way out of this invisible killing cage he'd been thrust into.

Karjakin was free to bask in the voluptuously protracted, soul-crushing period of time it took the highest-rated chess player in history to come to terms with the helpless, dead-end void he'd been given. It was a deliverance and an apotheosis of everything that Karjakin had ever worked for, overcome, dreamed, and sacrificed for.

In the end, Carlsen was unable to stop one of Karjakin's

innocuous pawns from strolling innocently enough into his malevolent promised land to emerge as an all-powerful, Lady Macbeth, vindictive-as-hell queen at the end of the board.

Carlsen took a last sip of water and struggled to swallow. He bowed his head and furrowed his brow in frustration. Finally, dejectedly, making no eye contact with Sergey, he offered his hand.

The hall erupted. After nearly forty hours at the board across eight games, the crowd finally had a clear verdict from one of the games. The rising tension had, for the briefest of moments, wrenched chess from the dominion computers had long claimed, ever since they dispensed with Kasparov via Deep Blue, and it reminded the world again of the game's fragile and majestic humanity.

Sergey accepted the brief handshake without a trace of relief, let alone extravagant euphoria. For the first time in twenty-one years, since he'd begun playing chess at five, he was finally on the verge of realizing his dream, a dream that required uprooting his entire family and abandoning the country of his birth. All he had to do was draw in the next four games and he would be champion of the world.

Each man signed his score sheet with his S. T. Dupont pen. Typically, each player hands their score sheet to the other to sign. Karjakin offered his across the board and the graveyard of his fallen pieces beside it. Carlsen neglected to extend the same courtesy. He got to his feet, spun around, and discovered he was facing not an exit but his own tragic reflection in the one-sided mirror.

For Magnus, the humiliation wasn't over. Karjakin led the way down a starkly lit hallway as Magnus, head bowed, exhausted and disoriented, lumbered clumsily behind. A reporter got to Karjakin and thrust a microphone in his face immediately after he emerged from the hallway. Carlsen, contractually obligated to join his opponent in postgame interviews, seethed while Karjakin fielded questions in English. Already boyish-looking, Karjakin seemed like a teenager who'd just finished his first date with a girl out of his league and somehow, against all odds, successfully gotten to second base. Though he spoke much more smoothly than at any time previously in the championship, his stammering, broken English made answering only a few softball questions take up more time than a distraught Carlsen could bear. When it was his turn to answer questions Carlsen brushed off the reporter and stormed past, urgently pacing toward the joint postgame press conference.

Karjakin was stopped by another reporter and dutifully answered more questions while Carlsen ignored pleas to talk with anyone and continued alone to the press conference. Because he'd forgone all interviews, when Carlsen got to his seat none of the organizers were ready for him. The moderator wasn't set up and Karjakin still hadn't finished. Carlsen sat waiting for his opponent to arrive while a horde of cameras and reporters took stock of his torment. Finally, Carlsen tossed up his hands in disgust, got to his feet, waved his arms around wildly to organizers, and stormed off.

His hysterical theatrics left the room silent. What's more, the chess fans and serious players in attendance knew that, in accordance with Carlsen's contract, he stood to lose more money from being fined 10 percent of his winnings from the championship than 99.9 percent of all competitive chess players around the world could hope to make through a year's work.

• • •

"Some of my demons I keep only to myself," Carlsen ominously confessed, during the world championship he won three years earlier, in 2013. "It's easiest that way. Because not sharing is usually easier than sharing. At least that's the way I feel. It is definitely a huge frustration to feel that you're the only one that understands something. . . . That's really the lonely part about being a chess player. It's all up to you. Always dealing with your own . . . demons and problems."

It was hard not to wonder: Were we now witnessing Carlsen precariously drawing closer to that edge hanging over Fischer's abyss than he had ever been in his life? And it wasn't just Fischer. Though his cautionary tale had defined chess at least as much as van Gogh's ear did art, I'd discovered in my research at the library so many stories of great chess players cracking up—their sparkling talent shattered like so many pieces of a fallen chandelier.

There was the great Paul Morphy. The headline of his *New York Times* obituary read: "The Great Chess Player Insane for Nearly a Score of Years." In 1859, after a year spent dominating Europe, Morphy, still just twenty-two, returned home an American hero and suddenly, mysteriously announced his retirement and plans to return to his law career in New Orleans. According to legend, Morphy ran his law practice into the ground by alienating his clients with obsessive rants about chess. After his practice went under, a mentally imploding Morphy wandered the streets of New Orleans, raging to himself about imagined enemies and maintaining conversations with invisible people until friends begged him to have himself committed to a local mental asylum. Morphy violently fought back and threatened to sue anyone who tried—friends, family, or the church. Myths abound that Morphy was found dead in his bathtub surrounded by a circle of women's shoes—which all gives "Morphy Mania" a very different meaning.

Then there's our old friend Wilhelm Steinitz. After his victory in the first world championship, he held the title for eight years. He would finally lose it in 1894, to Emanuel Lasker, who was thirty-two years younger. The age disparity between the two is still the largest in championship history. Like most chess greats, Steinitz didn't exactly take losing well. In 1897, age sixty-one, he played a rematch with Lasker in Moscow and was soundly defeated. Soon after, he suffered a complete mental collapse and was institutionalized inside a Moscow sanatorium for forty days. During his confinement, Steinitz incessantly challenged fellow patients to games of chess. By the time of his death three years later, he was bragging about playing chess with God over an invisible telephone. "It is not without significance that the death of Steinitz should have been due to mental disorder," wrote the *New York Times*. "His death seems to be another admonition that 'serious chess' is a very serious thing indeed."

Lasker lost his world-champion crown in 1921, in Havana, to José Capablanca. Four years later, Lasker lost to the young Mexican grandmaster Carlos Torre—who implemented such a transcendently beautiful queen sacrifice that the combination was immortalized in chess history as "the Windmill." Only a year later, possibly driven to do so by his fiancée's sending him a Dear John letter, Torre stripped naked on a Fifth Avenue bus. He was institutionalized. After being released, he returned to Mexico, never played competitive chess again, and spent the majority of his remaining life hospitalized for mental illness. His close friend Dr. Carlos Fruvas Garnica blamed his breakdown on the demands chess placed on him.

During the Russian Revolution, Aron Nimzowitsch, one of the world's best chess players in his time and a seminal chess writer, avoided military service by *pretending* to be crazy, complaining of an invisible fly on his head. Polish grandmaster Savielly Tartakower remarked that Nimzowitsch "pretends to be crazy in order to drive us all crazy." But before too long, Nimzowitsch's habit of jumping on tables after losing or doing headstands for no reason between moves was suspected to be the genuine article. At restaurants, he was obsessed with the belief that *all* waiters had conspired to serve him smaller portions than were offered other customers and he'd throw enormous tantrums protesting this injustice no matter what was done to placate his ravings.

In 1901, elite German chess player Johannes Minckwitz threw himself under a train. In 1932, Polish master Akiba Rubinstein retired from chess citing pathological shyness; he soon battled debilitating paranoia that led him to spend his last thirty years institutionalized. Raymond Weinstein grew up in the same neighborhood as Bobby Fischer and went to the same high school. He came in third at the 1961 US championship, where he and Fischer competed against each other. Whether it was because he was competing against a talent as otherworldly as Fischer—Weinstein never officially beat Fischer, though he did achieve one draw—or something else, he too eventually snapped. First he attacked a chess writer in Amsterdam and was deported back to New York. Then, in 1964, living in a halfway house, the twenty-three-year-old Weinstein got in an argument with his eighty-three-year-old roommate and sliced the old man's throat with a barber's razor, leaving him to die. Weinstein was deemed incompetent to stand trial and was remanded to Kirby Forensic Psychiatric Center.

Even more violent was Claude Frizzel Bloodgood, born Klaus Frizzel Bluttgutt III in La Paz, Mexico, in 1937 (some sources date his birth back to 1924). Some hustlers on the street had told me about him. Bloodgood started off innocently enough: as a teenager in the 1950s he gained attention for hustling—or maybe *lying* about hustling—Humphrey Bogart, Gary Cooper, and Charlie Chaplin, among many other Hollywood elite. He tried and failed to use these connections to break into acting or writing for Hollywood. In the late 1950s he headed south and founded the All Service Postal Chess Club and was editor of the *Virginia Chess News Roundup*. He was a rating statistician for the Virginia State Chess Association.

Then he made the natural progression into burglary in the 1960s. After serving time in a Delaware prison for one of his burglary convictions, he emerged only to take up forgery, namely that of his parents' signatures. His parents reported Bloodgood for cashing their IRS check. Bloodgood's father's resolve to put his son in jail wavered before the trial, and he died suddenly, possibly owing to stress. His widow, on the other hand, had no conflicts of conscience. She went to court to offer her testimony and her son responded by informing her in the courtroom, "You'll never live to spend Dad's money." In 1969, after Bloodgood had served a year in prison, true to his word, he returned home to beat his mother to death with a baseball bat, roll her body up into a carpet, and dump her in Virginia's Great Dismal Swamp. He was sentenced to death. In 1972, the US Supreme Court commuted his sentence to one of life imprisonment. He began playing thousands of chess games by mail. Two years later, Bloodgood and a fellow inmate received a furlough from prison to play in a chess tournament and overpowered the guard to escape, only to be captured soon after. He returned to prison and played chess there and via correspondence. Bloodgood played ten sustained games with one correspondent in England that took up to twenty-eight years. He also published three books from jail on chess gambits. Without ever winning a title, he apparently managed to achieve a rating as high as 2789 (more than qualifying for a grandmaster title) while in prison. In 1996 he was ranked second in the country by the US Chess Federation. Like Fischer, Bloodgood lived a year for each square on the chessboard, before dying in prison at age sixty-four, in 2001.

To some extent, I wondered if there might be a parallel with the greatest matadors of Spain—nearly all of whom died or came within inches of doing so. Bullfighting aficionados expect their geniuses to accept greater danger the more capable they become. The quality of art and emotional impact in bullfighting—a tragedy by design, covered next to opera in the culture pages of Spain's newspapers—is predicated not on the murder of bulls, but on the willingness of matadors to allow death ever closer as they dance with the hero of the tragedy, the bull. The more you pay to watch a matador, the closer the bull's horn is expected to come to the man's heart with each pass. Perhaps, like bullfighters, the greatest geniuses of chess are also required to risk too much of themselves in the pursuit of perfection. For matadors it's their bodies. For chess players it's their minds.

And yet of all those players mentioned, none of them had a stranger, sadder story than the guy Frank Brady would tell me about.

# 9

# "I AM UNUSUAL, A LITTLE."

Frank Brady was eighty-two, he'd just undergone a series of treatments for macular degeneration, and his hip was bothering him, but none of that was slowing him down. Not with a world championship taking place in his hometown. He showed up to the championship each day dressed in a dapper suit and full of energy. I don't think I saw anyone those two weeks who seemed to be enjoying themselves more. He knew everyone, and he couldn't move five feet without someone stopping him to talk. As Fischer's biographer, founding editor of *Chess Life* magazine, former secretary of the United States Chess Federation and past president of the Marshall Chess Club, the guy was a walking candy factory of delicious chess anecdotes, gossip, and history. (And his interests weren't limited to chess. He'd taught journalism at several New

York area universities, including Columbia and St. John's, and had written biographies of Aristotle Onassis, Barbra Streisand, Orson Welles, and Hugh Hefner. He'd even worked for Hefner at *Playboy* earlier in his career.)

Earlier in the championship, I finally caught him unoccupied for a moment and asked him the one question no one had been able to answer.

"Do you remember Bobby and Kubrick playing together at the Marshall at any point?" I asked.

"I'm sure they played," he said. "Bobby was always there. Stanley came by nearly every week to the Marshall. It was round-robin tournaments when he dropped by. They definitely would have played. Stanley was impossible to forget."

"Why?" I asked.

"He'd *never* pay his fucking dues!" Brady said, then howled with laughter. "I'd always have to hound him and he'd reply the same way whenever he came in, 'You can take it out of my winnings.' The arrogant prick."

Brady had told me to swing by the Marshall Chess Club so he could show me the place and we could talk more. The day after Magnus's shocking loss in game eight was an off day, so I took Brady up on his invitation.

The Marshall Chess Club owned the brownstone at 23 West Tenth Street in the extravagantly wealthy Greenwich Village neighborhood and had celebrated its one hundredth anniversary the year before. There are more than five hundred current members who are welcome seven days a week. Membership for New York residents is $325 a year and less for younger or more accomplished players. There are tournaments most nights—three or four hundred a year, Brady had told me—and frequently many incredibly talented masters and grandmasters are available to give lessons. What the old Yankee Stadium represented to a dynasty of baseball's legendary players, the Marshall was to a host of the twentieth century's great American chess players. Despite Frank Marshall being one of the game's most elite players, his attitude toward all chess players was overwhelmingly welcoming and inclusive. While Marshall was widely regarded as the most beloved of all chess masters, you could feel inside his club that he loved players with even more affection than he received. A hundred framed portraits of players adorn the interior in celebration of their contributions to chess. When you arrive and look over the faces and level of comfort and familiarity members have with this place, it's clear that wherever they go after the Marshall closes shop at night, this is their true second home; they live here and are welcomed like family. Brady's bias and paternal warmth toward all chess players is palpable.

New York chess legend Asa Hoffmann was there the night I showed up. I recognized him from photographs and interviews he had given in documentaries. Hoffmann was a go-to subject for outsiders seeking to understand the dark allure of chess, largely on the basis of the New York City, upper-crust, lucky-sperm-club, born-on-third-base life he gave up to pursue the game as chess's peculiar answer to Fast Eddie Felson. He was two weeks older than Fischer, seventy-three now, and physically slight, but Hoffmann, even sitting alone at a chessboard staring at a portrait of the young Fischer hanging on the wall, filled the whole building with his personality. He was as keen to talk about his gambling exploits with backgammon and bridge or Scrabble and poker as he was to talk about chess. He began talking about four hundred different mostly worthless things he was trying to sell (chess antiques, signed first editions of his book *Chess Gladiator*, clocks, copies of a 1987 *New York Times* profile on him, etc.). I was never fully able to understand why exactly he was selling them, beyond the compulsion of any social interaction needing to collide with commerce. Within five minutes, unprompted, Hoffmann raised the subject of money at least fifty times with the same wry chuckle trailing off each time. And yet, Hoffmann, the son of Park Avenue lawyers, educated at Hunter College Elementary, Horace Mann, and Columbia—some of the finest institutions in the country—against his parents' wishes had abandoned their hope of becoming a lawyer and dropped out of Columbia to devote himself to chess full-time.

"Explain this to me," I said.

Hoffmann shrugged.

"I mean, my uncle was a big-shot Harvard lawyer. My parents wanted me to go down that path also. But I *ended up* earning a million dollars here and there on the chessboard. Sure, never tournaments. Never made virtually *anything* at tournaments despite winning numerous times throughout my life. But five dollars here and there at blitz?"

"You made a million dollars *here and there* hustling speed chess?" I interjected.

"Before computers took that market away, it was possible. Washington Square? Liberty Park next to the World Trade Center? Sure. I earned a million dollars. It just took me fifty years to do it. I probably averaged twenty grand a year overall. But remember! There's no taxes on that."

Brady and his wife of fifty years, Maxine, strolled into the back room of the Marshall. Maxine was a writer herself and the author of *The Monopoly Book: Strategy and Tactics of the World's Most Popular Game.* Maxine pulled a book from the library and sat in the corner quietly reading while her husband bought a Diet Coke from the vending machine and came over with careful steps to the free chair next to the chess table where I was sitting. I could tell from the way he squinted in the glare of the light in the room that he'd had another round of injections for his macular degeneration.

He sat down.

"So are you going to play in the tournament tonight?" Brady asked me.

"Are *you*?" I said.

"I always have an excuse why not to play," he said, smiling sheepishly. "I like to win games, but losing them? The balance is not there anymore at my age. It still gets to me."

"How do you think Magnus feels after last night?" I asked.

"He took that loss hard. The press conference also. That was quite a performance he gave."

"Only four games left," I said. "You think he'll bounce back?"

Brady smiled.

"He should. But then . . . you never know."

And then he proceeded to tell me the story of how he met Fischer. I wasn't sure how many thousands of times Brady had told the story, but from Maxine's reassuring smirk it was a lot. Yet it was clear he'd still yet to get the wrapping paper off. When he talked about Fischer his eyes lit up in a way they didn't when he talked about anyone else, even as his voice revealed some lingering sadness playing with his emotions. Brady was still interested in the chess world, but you could tell that since Fischer, nothing had ever been quite as interesting.

Brady first encountered Bobby Fischer in 1955 at a tournament being played only four blocks away. Fischer was twelve and Brady was twenty-one. They became fast friends. A year later, on October 17, 1956, Fischer played his "Game of the Century" at the Marshall against 1953 US Open champion Donald Byrne. After a minor mistake by Byrne on the eleventh move, Fischer mystified observers with a queen sacrifice six moves later. As Fischer gradually devoured Byrne's rook, both his bishops, and a pawn in exchange for the queen, the crowd, and Byrne, slowly got wise to Fischer's miraculous method at work. As Fischer closed in for a checkmate, Byrne's queen was forced to remain idle and useless on the opposite side of the board.

Brady was an ally and close friend to a man who made one of the oddest and most spectacular ascents in American culture. Brady was with Fischer at the Marshall in 1965 when Fischer remotely played by teletype in the Havana-based Capablanca Memorial tournament. Fischer had been offered $3,000 to show up in Havana to compete, but the US Department of State refused to allow him to travel as tensions continued to simmer between Cuba and the United States after the April 17, 1961, Bay of Pigs invasion and the October 1962 Cuban Missile Crisis that brought the world closer to the brink of nuclear annihilation than at any other point before or since. Dr. José Raúl Capablanca Jr., son of the tournament's namesake and one of Fischer's cherished chess heroes, relayed Fischer's moves in Havana. Despite the ridiculous circumstances in which Fischer was forced to compete, he placed fourth. The same year as the Capablanca Memorial, Brady wrote *Profile of a Prodigy*, the first-ever biography of the twenty-two-year-old Fischer. As a courtesy, Brady allowed Fischer to see the manuscript before publication. Fischer immediately objected to being identified as a Jew in the book. It was his only objection. Brady explained to Fischer that, under Talmudic law, Bobby was Jewish owing to his Jewish mother, Regina. "I don't give a crap about Talmudic law," Fischer replied. Fischer ended their friendship based on this dispute.

Sadly, going back as far as his teenage years, Fischer had made anti-Semitic remarks, and one account I read noted that he cherished a color photograph that he kept of Adolf Hitler. Brady loathed this side of Fischer, but interestingly refused to attribute it in any way to being a by-product of mental illness. He held Fischer entirely responsible, lamenting, "Bobby just went . . . *rotten.*"

In many ways the Marshall felt like a loving parent's shrine dedicated to Fischer. Lush black-and-white photographs and news clippings from Fischer's youth were on all the walls. Yet there wasn't any artifact *after* 1972 that I could find. Fischer's post-1972 legacy's omission haunted the rooms as much as anything present.

I asked Brady if he had ever point-blank asked Bobby Fischer about losing. Brady's eyes lit up and he smiled bashfully. "I certainly did ask him that question once. Once and only once. And I remember *exactly* what he said in response. He looked up from the board where we were playing and shouted, 'Don't *ever* ask me about losing! Don't *ever* ask me again!'"

"After Fischer refused to defend his title and went into hiding, who was the next young American player who came along that really resonated as the *next* Fischer? Was there anybody like him?"

"We had some strong players who came up where I'm sure the comparison was spoken of out loud," Brady said.

I was still thinking of Magnus and the abyss.

"Did any of those players after Fischer, carrying the burden of becoming the *next* Fischer, crack under the pressure?"

An older gentleman, who had been eavesdropping from another table at which a young chess player's mother was talking, spoke a name in a tone befitting a séance: "Peter Winston."

A silence spread out over the room, as though we were picking at a ghostly scab.

"Peter Winston," Brady agreed solemnly. "Yes. Quite true."

"Who's Peter Winston?" I asked.

"Very talented player from New York," Brady said. "Two years after Fischer won the world title, Winston shared first prize at the 1974 US Junior Championships. And he was a math prodigy even before he was a chess prodigy. Peter got a lot of attention in 1972, when he was fourteen, beating Walter Browne, who was then the six-time national champion. That got people talking. He absolutely *crushed* Browne."

"What happened to him after that?" I asked.

"Well . . ." Brady took a breath and played with his beard for a second. "You can go in the other room and talk to Jay Bonin. Very fine chess player. Probably the most active chess player in the country. He's an international master. He was one of the last people to see Peter during a tournament at Hunter College High School on the Upper East Side in the winter of 1977. Bonin was playing there too. Winston had been institutionalized for a time. He dabbled in illicit drugs. Things had been deteriorating with him for a while and he became somewhat unhinged. The medication he was taking was also having a lot of negative effects. He'd go off it and perhaps it was even worse for him. Peter went to that tournament and played nine straight games against vastly inferior competition. But he still managed to lose each and every game. He vanished soon after that during one of the worst recorded blizzards in New York City. He left behind his money and ID, and walked out into that blizzard, and his body has never been found. He was only twenty when he disappeared."

From the other table, the stranger added, "If indeed he *did* kill himself, Peter would have made sure his body would never be found."

"I never met Peter myself," Brady confessed. "He disappeared in 1978. I first read about him in the *Saturday Evening Post* in 1964 or 1965. They did a cover story about child genius and there was a profile on him in that issue. He was six and from Sands Point Elementary in Long Island, a school for gifted kids, and Peter was the one who stood out with his ability in math. His father was a professor at Columbia but he died young. A heart attack or something. I think Peter wasn't even ten yet. They lived up on Riverside Drive next to Columbia."

A large man in spectacles, maybe sixty, ducked his head into the room to say hello to Brady and his wife.

"Jay," Brady said. "Hold on one second, if you would. Brin here would like to talk to you for a second about Peter Winston. You played him at Hunter College High School at the last tournament he played, isn't that right?"

Bonin nodded his head.

"He went zero and nine," he said. "I was there. Almost forty years ago. My God, that's scary. Nobody knows for sure where he is now. He disappeared. I assume he committed suicide. He *could* be institutionalized somewhere. Peter had such a tragic life.

He was such a talented player. I didn't know him terribly well. We played here a few times. The tournament's starting downstairs. I have to go."

"Good luck tonight," Brady smiled.

Bonin adjusted his glasses.

"You too," he said, "if you ever start playing again."

Brady turned back to me.

"About six years ago," he said, "totally out of the blue, a woman named Florence called me. It was Peter's mother. This was thirty-two years after he disappeared. She told me she had a lot of chess stuff and would I like to come up and look at it. I could have whatever I wanted. I brought Maxine and an intern I had working with me up to her apartment on Riverside. We met the mother, only for a few minutes. Very sweet person. She was moving. She had to move. It was a Columbia University–owned apartment. She had to get out. She led me to a room in the apartment, and the strange thing was, all of Peter's clothes were there. This was over thirty years after he disappeared and it looked like he was just going to come in that night and go to sleep."

"Totally preserved?" I asked.

"Totally preserved," Brady said. "She told us she didn't enter the room at all. It wasn't a very big room, very basic but comfortable for one person. Mostly books. I took almost all the chess books, maybe four or five boxes at least. And we brought them here to the Marshall. We used to have lots of book sales. Almost right after the phone call from Peter's mother, I found out she died."

We said nothing for a moment.

"Chess has these kinds of extraordinary characters," Brady said.

• • •

"BOY GENIUS," the cover of the December 19, 1964, issue of the *Saturday Evening Post* proclaims. And inside, in Gilbert Millstein's profile on Peter Jonathan Winston, titled "The Remarkable Life of a Little Genius," the first thing we learn about the six-year-old Winston is that he is "alarmingly bright" yet "far more human—and fascinating—than the stereotypical child prodigy." Little Winston is shown in a series of photographs, drawing math diagrams, arguing with teachers, and working with his mother on his homework.

Not long after Winston first enrolled at his school for gifted children on Long Island at the age of five, the headmaster, Benjamin Fine, a former education editor of the *New York Times*, asked him when his birthday was: "March 18, 1958," Winston answered. Then he asked Fine the same thing, though quickly qualifying that he was only interested in the month and day, not the year. We can only imagine how the adults who observed this exchange might have reacted. Fine told him his birthday was on September 1.

"You're lucky," Peter responded. "Daddies can come to your party."

"What do you mean?" Fine asked.

"Well, your birthday's on a Sunday," Winston replied. "It's not a working day. But next year it's going to be on a Tuesday. Normally it would have been on a Monday, but 1964 will be a leap year."

Fine blinked at Winston before turning to the parents in the room. "I *heard* him, all right. But I'm not sure I *believe* it."

So Fine and the parents consulted an almanac to confirm Winston's accuracy. More adults stepped up to have him perform the same magic trick. Winston obliged—he had already taught himself to make the snap calculation for any year between 1800 and 2000—before changing the subject to a more interesting discussion with Fine about positive and negative numbers.

In the profile, Peter is described as "intense-looking," and one faculty member remarked that he looked "coiled." The big-eared boy was prone to temper tantrums. The six-year-old Winston is quoted within the first hundred words of the article as confessing, "I think I have a sickness that only I know about and nobody else can understand. . . . I don't think I know how to love."

Over the weekend following President John F. Kennedy's assassination, Winston intensely prepared a presentation for school on Monday, inventorying in great detail the shooting with information culled from hours spent scouring newspapers and watching television. He delivered his own epic eulogy for Kennedy in front of teachers and classmates.

"The fact is," Gilbert Millstein writes, "that Peter Winston is not simply an intellectually gifted child. He is clearly a prodigy, and if intelligence tests are any criterion, at the heady level of genius." Indeed, the clinical psychologist who tested Winston for admission into the school concluded, "Peter is a true genius. He is 5 yrs. and 5 mos. and his range of information, arithmetical reasoning, attention, concentration and abstract reasoning is equivalent to 15 yrs. and 10 mos."

Yet Peter's lack of coordination was noted in his inability to even properly hold a pencil. This, combined with his "merely average" scores on judgment tests, restricted his soaring scores elsewhere from "pressing against the maximum" frontiers of genius.

Winston was also nearly as famous at school for his free spirit and eccentric behavior. He still slept in a crib in his parents' bedroom. He refused any food at Sands Point Elementary. He struggled with an inability to relate to classmates. He kissed hands. When a child joined him in a sandbox, Winston would break the ice by declaring the latest symphony his mother had played him. He desperately wanted to get along with other children, but didn't seem to know how. His sadness and aggression became noted traits early on, overshadowed by his total powers of absorption with subjects he became obsessed with. He could read at two. Mastered fractions at three. At six he memorized the names, ages, and terms of office of every president, along with the names, capitals and populations of all fifty states and the exact date they entered the union.

"How come you're so interested in me?" Winston asks the reporter at one point in the interview. But he already knows the answer, yet carefully underplays it. "I am unusual, a little."

"My husband, Leonard, says we're like the poor fisherman and his wife who were given a gem," Winston's mother explained. "We don't quite know what to do with this gem. We haven't got any plans for Peter. We just want him to be happy. . . . Maybe he won't be able to make use of this vast potential; maybe something will get in the way. But I have hopes that nothing will. I'm not fearful for him, but I am protective. A few weeks ago, when he was going to sleep, he said to me, 'Do you want me to be famous?' I said no."

Between the time this *Saturday Evening Post* profile was published and Winston's father died suddenly from a heart attack, chess entered Winston's life and exercised a tremendous hold over the prodigiously talented child. His father had expressly discouraged his son from playing chess, afraid, according to a source close to the family who spoke with me but asked not to be identified, "he'd grab it and run. He wanted him to remain with his true gift, which was *math*. Peter's grandfather taught him chess and his dad was not happy." Winston's father's fears about chess taking over his son's life proved all too warranted.

Soon after his father's death, the brilliance of Winston's games were being written up in magazines. Before he was old enough to qualify for a driver's license, Random House approached him with a book contract to explore chess. But already his stability and mental health were also increasingly becoming an issue. He frequently abandoned his schoolwork and, still in his teens, cofounded an *alternative* high school. By some accounts, like many youths in America at that time, he dabbled in LSD, and this potentially exacerbated his struggles to keep a grip on his life. He openly complained of feeling burned out and coping with intense feelings of alienation.

In 1974, at the US Junior Championships, Winston, only sixteen, tied for first place after playing to a draw in the final against future grandmaster Larry Christiansen. Winston was offered an opportunity to play in the World Junior Championships in Manila and accepted.

In Manila, despite his best efforts, Winston was unable to muster anything but a discouraging sixth place. Two years later, back in New York in 1976, age eighteen, he was hospitalized and diagnosed as schizophrenic. Psychiatric issues led Winston to repeatedly, voluntarily, and with increasing urgency, return to mental hospitals, where he was given heavy doses of dangerous, mind-altering medication and often left in padded rooms. His diagnosis was later switched to one of manic depression. Winston would emerge from treatment complaining that his medication had tampered with his mind and fouled up his cognitive functions.

He returned to the sanctuary of chess outside institution walls and discovered that his game had deteriorated immensely, perhaps triggering further fears that the deterioration was irrevocable. Winston entered tournaments and was dominated by opponents whose ability was vastly inferior to his own, as previously exhibited. On top of whatever prescribed medication Winston was taking, according to several people who knew him that I interviewed, he experimented with illicit drugs also. As he struggled to keep his life together, friends noted with alarm and deep concern that he abandoned any semblance of basic hygiene. He rarely bathed or slept.

In late 1977, as winter took hold in New York, Winston entered the Hunter College High School tournament and lost those nine games in succession. For a player rated as highly as Winston, this created a controversy. An administrator from FIDE ventured that the possibility of a player of Winston's caliber losing all his games at the tournament was so statistically remote that instead the most likely scenario was that Winston had lost them intentionally. Officials refused to rate the tournament results. After losing his final series of games, Winston allegedly threw away all the medication he had been prescribed for his manic depression disorder.

One night not long after, in January 1978, according to Sarah Weinman's 2012 report in the *New York Observer*, Winston called his sister Wynde to plead with her to pick him up from a racetrack at the Meadowlands in New Jersey and bring him back to her apartment in Manhattan. Wynde agreed and drove off into the night only to find her brother severely distressed. She brought him back to her apartment to sleep. When Peter awoke, his sister offered her apartment for as long as Winston needed on the condition that he immediately see a doctor. Winston wasted no time responding to the offer and ran screaming out the door without even gathering his jacket. He had no money or belongings with him.

Winston headed to an unidentified friend's apartment. The friend was with his family eating lunch when Winston deliriously spoke of fleeing to Texas to meet with Walter Korn, a seventy-year-old author who had most notably written several revised editions of *Modern Chess Openings*, which many tournament players considered essential reading. Winston described Korn as "God." The friend's parents were so troubled by Winston's state that they called his mother.

Winston left the apartment before his mother or anyone else could do anything and wandered out into one of the most notorious blizzards to have ever struck New York. The storm shut down traffic from as far as Virginia all the way north to Maine. Winston was six weeks shy of his twentieth birthday. According to Weinman's reporting, the NYPD has no record of anyone named Peter Winston disappearing, and his Social Security number has never seen any activity since.

Where this gets extra spooky is that when I filed a Freedom of Information Law request with the NYPD, they denied my request on the basis that the case was still open. I appealed, given that it's going on forty years since Winston disappeared, and was denied again. This time the NYPD said they had no records related to Peter Winston. Also, while most information publicly available related to Winston's disappearance dates him walking out into a blizzard in late January, the actual *blizzard* of 1978 formed on February 5 and broke on February 7. A source I talked to who was close to the family, and who had never before gone on record about Winston's disappearance, was categorical that the last time they saw him alive was during the blizzard in an apartment on Tenth Street and Fifth Avenue, just above Washington Square Park. They also assured me a missing-person report had indeed been filed with the police and that private investigators were hired by the family to track Winston down. When everything failed, a psychic was even consulted.

Weinman suggests that on the remote chance Winston is alive, he may have been discovered during that winter storm and placed in an asylum. Or he may be buried in a potter's field on Hart Island—131 acres at the western end of the Long Island Sound—where 550 indigent corpses remain unidentified. The Hart Island cemetery is the largest tax-funded graveyard on earth. Over a million people are buried on the island. I put in requests there too for possible information about Winston, and came back with another dead end.

After learning of D. T. Max's March 21, 2011, *New Yorker* profile of the rising then-twenty-year-old chess sensation Magnus Carlsen, fellow *New Yorker* writer and film critic Richard Brody was immediately taken fifty-three years back to when he first encountered Peter Winston, at the age of five, at Sands Point Academy. He wrote about their relationship in *The New Yorker* on St. Patrick's Day, the day before Winston's fifty-third birthday. Brody remembered Winston as "the only true, epochal genius I'd ever met," and Magnus Carlsen's journey "brought up a painful riot of memories," Brody wrote. "I played lots of chess as a child and through adolescence, largely due to the electrifying personal influence of one childhood friend, whose story, as it turns out, is a horrifying mystery."

When the *Saturday Evening Post* mentioned Winston arguing with a fellow classmate about the existence of God, Brody was that unnamed child. Brody learned chess at the age of seven and regularly played with, and was crushed by, the prodigiously talented Winston. From the start, Brody was in awe of Winston and his "sublime insolence" that once led a teacher to threaten to hurl a rock through Winston's skull. For the next five years the two became very close, until going their separate ways at different schools around the age of eleven. The last news Brody heard of Winston was that Winston had tied for the US Junior Championship in 1974.

Years later, long after Winston had disappeared during the snowstorm at the end of January 1978, Brody tried searching for details of what had become of his old friend, only to discover deeply troubling, vague accounts online of the circumstances of Winston's deterioration.

Brody concluded his article darkly. "Playing chess in any serious manner is the best way for a young person to avoid facing the sort of complex interpersonal experience that is the most essential kind of learning that's needed to help a person make his way in the world. I think of the time I spent on chess as worse than a distraction or a waste—a pathological delusion."

I reached out to Richard Brody and asked him some questions about both Peter Winston and his thoughts on chess.

"I think that chess itself is a very troubling game for geniuses and for ordinary people, and perhaps much more for ordinary people," he told me. "The analogy I would make is to Plato's *Republic*: Socrates talks about how philosophy is important for young people to work on, but that young people should first have experience with the more practical side of life, adult life, adult responsibility, and then when they are worldly and generally experienced, then they're ready for philosophy. Or, rather, they are raised to the level of life experience that makes them worthy of philosophy. Philosophy is too real and too perfect. If you study philosophy when you're young, it spoils you for experience, which spoils experience for you. It actually makes you think the realm of ideas and the realm of books is better, worthier, than the realm of life that one experiences. A young person who has an imagination and energy and is given good books of philosophy as a teenager will never go out and live. And that is terrible. And chess is the *same*."

"Could you tell me about meeting Peter for the first time?" I asked.

"It was September 1963, we were both five, and everybody else had short hair. Not crew cuts, but short hair. Peter had floppy hair. Everybody else wore nondescript clothing, middle-class clothing. There was something bohemian about Peter's clothing even then. His shoes were a little different. His shirts were different—a little more rumpled. His father was a professor at Columbia. His mother taught also. His parents were intellectuals. Everybody else there came from the suburbs. Peter wasn't from the suburbs.

"The *Saturday Evening Post*, a very popular magazine at the time, sent a reporter into school that year. When it came out in September, it was a profile of a young genius."

"And it was your friend Peter," I said.

"Yes," Brody said. "It was Peter. Our fathers would take Peter and me to the Museum of Natural History or to go hear [Leonard] Bernstein conduct the [New York] Philharmonic, that sort of thing. I had visited his apartment a few times at that point. He was insolent in a lovely way. He was very plainspoken but he didn't smile a lot. He wasn't dour, but his remarks were sharp, cutting; as I recollect he didn't have a hell of a lot of respect for authority even then. But not in a negative way. It became a bit of a problem as he got older. One science teacher who took exception to Peter's cutting remarks used to yell at him and even hurled chalk at him."

"When do you remember chess entering your lives?" I asked.

"I don't remember chess until second or third grade. Peter and I played at seven or eight and he trounced me. He would give me queen odds and still destroy me."

"Did that hurt?" I asked.

"Not at all." Brody laughed. "Didn't hurt me at all. I mean, we all recognized Peter's genius. I already knew that he was different from the rest of us, in a very good way. And his father died soon after. Dropped dead of a heart attack. What its effect on him emotionally was, I don't know. Kids don't talk that way. I didn't and he didn't. But what I knew from my parents was that it had a significant economic effect, that he went from a middle-class kid to a poor kid *overnight*. From then on, whenever we did stuff with Peter and his mother came along and my father was there, my father always picked up the check. That sort of thing. We weren't rich, but we were middle-class.

"And then in sixth grade our little group dispersed suddenly. I went to a suburban public school and Peter went to a private school. I think I saw him once or twice after that. It was pleasant but the thread was kind of cut. Then I followed his exploits in chess, because I was still playing chess. I was still the best local player, and I would read chess magazines where 'Winston wins *this* tournament.' 'Winston wins *that* tournament.' 'Winston rising star.' 'Winston wins US Junior Championship.' I was really kind of delighted for him."

"And Bobby Fischer was exploding at the same time and taking chess with him," I said.

"Fischer was exploding at the same time. That's right. Peter won the US Junior Championship only two years after Fischer won in Iceland."

"And America was rabidly chess-crazy?" I asked.

Brody laughed.

"America was chess-crazy. Did Peter himself dream that he would be another Fischer? I think people know their limits. He wasn't playing at Fischer-like levels. He *must* have known."

"Do you remember first hearing the rumor that Peter had disappeared?" I asked.

"I vaguely remember hearing a rumor about Peter having vanished and thinking that it was crazy," Brody said. "This was the age before the internet. A story I heard was that he walked out of that last tournament he played without a coat and walked out to some bridge and was never seen again. I don't know how the Peter I knew became the person that disappeared. I knew two stories that weirdly seemed inconsistent with each other. The kid I knew and ultimately what happened. And for the little bits and pieces of information I had in between, they didn't add up one way or the other. His adolescence and upbringing was obviously different than mine. He came from much more sophisticated people than I did. In a certain way I knew that he was, it's putting it funny, living a much more interesting life than I was. He was enjoying freedoms far wider than those that I enjoyed. I wasn't judgmental about it at all. I admired him. As much as I considered him a genius of math and chess, I sort of considered him a genius of life. I don't know that he read more than I did, but he read more widely than I did. He traveled. His imagination was far less inhibited and conventional. He had a very free mind. Even though his world experience wasn't enormous, I considered him far more worldly than me."

"And what about after chess took over?" I asked.

"That's the paradox, because as I came to understand, chess is a narrowing thing, not a broadening thing. Anybody is lucky to have one gift. Peter had one *enormous* gift that manifested itself in so many different ways. He was a vast mind attached to a vast character. He had a paradigm-changing intelligence. He wouldn't just respond to a new argument; he'd create a new category. I remember when Peter would play chess, like for fun, and something came out. It was like a different, ferocious side of his character. It came out when he discussed chess."

"Are you convinced Peter is dead?" I asked.

"Why would I be?" Brody said. "If he froze to death in the street during that blizzard, why wasn't he found? You know, what I heard way back is Peter disappeared. So the only story I ever heard subsequently is, he left that chess tournament. I don't know how, if I wanted to, I could disappear. I wouldn't know how to do it. How to leave my life without a trace. When I was younger I used to fantasize. I actually thought about it. That I wanted to do it, but I imagined, how would you do it? I literally don't know. And I'm guessing it's easier to imagine how to kill yourself than it is to imagine how to disappear. Was Peter's disappearance a spur-of-the-moment thing or premeditated? But I don't believe his mother, Florence, would have stopped looking for him. I can't believe that she would not have made an exceptional effort to find out if he was alive. That she wouldn't comb every hospital on the continent."

Because I knew Winston's mother was dead, I tracked down Peter Winston's sister, Wynde Juliet Winston, in Maryland, where she operates a law practice. I spoke with her for ten minutes about the possibility of her sharing her memories of her brother. She hadn't been pleased by what had been written about him and was wounded by numerous inaccuracies perpetuated about him. I liked her immediately and quickly felt ashamed to be bothering her. Before I was born, my mother lost an infant son to crib death and it stained the identity of our family in strange ways I'm still working through. But the way Wynde had lost her brother was unfathomably traumatic and damaging. We ended our conversation with her politely telling me that after forty years she still wasn't sure if she was ready to talk about Peter. From the tone of her voice, she hadn't come very far from the first day of losing him.

# 10

# QUEEN JUDIT

The morning of game nine, Sergey strode into the Fulton Market looking confident, relaxed, even cheerful. Magnus's face, on the other hand, betrayed the strain he had been under. He was un-shaven and looked pale, fatigued, and hungover from the effects of the previous loss. Playing with white pieces, having gone all-out for the win in game eight, he had dismissed chances for a draw and gravely blundered his way to a loss. Another loss this late in the match would almost surely bury his hopes of survival.

And yet, to the surprise of the assembled observers, he played this game even more aggressively. After Karjakin opened, Carlsen came out with an unusual variation known as the Archangel. The Archangel was developed in early 1960s by players from the north Russian town of Arkhangelsk, and I overheard two grandmasters say it requires a brain-melting degree of knowledge to carry off. They speculated that Carlsen had prepared it as a backup in his main arsenal of defenses. Carlsen was gambling that Karjakin's preparation did not include this variation and that he could be caught off guard. But Karjakin navigated it comfortably and by the twenty-third move had placed Carlsen at a critical juncture where he immediately plunged into thought and ate into his time. Karjakin tensely clung to a slight advantage for the next fifteen moves. Carlsen retreated a knight, and Karjakin, as if smelling blood, methodically spent twenty-six minutes ruminating on the best means of attack. When he finally picked his spot and boldly invaded Carlsen's enemy territory, grabbing a pawn and sacrificing a bishop, the crowd at the Fulton Market was so stunned to see the defensive genius uncharacteristically going for the kill against the wounded champion that a roaring cheer rang out.

Glancing around the hall, you could see the Magnus supporters taking a deep breath and looking distressed. But Karjakin was unable to apply sufficient pressure. While computer chess engines found an obscenely complex path to victory, Karjakin couldn't locate it on his own. Instead, the game steered toward a draw. By the forty-fourth move, it was finally clear that Carlsen's defense against Karjakin's attack would ensure he would not lose his second game in a row. But that didn't mean Karjakin was ready to concede a draw. They continued to play for a total of six hours and seventy-four moves until both accepted a draw. Carlsen, with uncharacteristic humility, teasingly confessed he was "just happy to survive" a game that likely would have ended his reign as world champion.

From the start, there was a palpable friction between chess journalists and reporters coming in to cover the story. The issue seemed to be something like the dynamic of C students having dibs on the story of A students. Complicating the issue further, the vast majority of top chess players had hardly been noted as academic powerhouses in their youth. Instead of books, all their attention had to be on the board. Many seemed to bear the familiar chip on the shoulder a lot of hyper-smart autodidacts carry through life. In any arena of ambition, status is paramount. But a cutthroat arena for supremely talented individuals that offered few rewards *beyond* status in the chess world was bound to leave many thin-skinned. Outsiders were treated a bit like eavesdroppers and Peeping Toms. In many instances, such a characterization wasn't all that inaccurate. Outsiders understandably struggled to find drama in the more technical elements of the game and as often as not explored the political backdrops or more lurid narratives behind chess players' lives for mainstream audiences. But how different was focusing on a chess player's private life, or stereotyping, or glibly conforming to one-note angles, from most art or sports coverage for mainstream audiences? In 1955, the British playwright and drama critic Kenneth Tynan controversially turned his attention to bullfighting. He wrote in the preface to his book *Bull Fever*: "No public spectacle in the world is more technical, offers less to the untaught observer, than a bullfight." Anybody from outside chess tasked with covering it discovers, with tremendous immediacy, it's highly doubtful Tynan ever had a high-level chess game caught in the crosshairs of his critical eye.

One chess grandmaster who for years regularly covered the game for online outlets lamented to me that he was regularly hit up for quotes and analyses about the game from outside journalists, yet none of their editors ever approached him to hire him to write

THE GRANDMASTER

163

the actual articles. Some of the chess journalists I came across treated the World Chess Championships with the seriousness of Bob Woodward and Carl Bernstein covering Watergate. Was that any different from *wine* journalists covering rare-wine auctions at which record prices were set? From art writers covering dealers and collectors at an auction of Damien Hirst's work at Christie's or Sotheby's? Maybe a lot of it came down to money also. On the occasions I've been afforded the luxury of being flown all over America and put up in a motel or hotel while I spend a week with a prominent boxer for a profile, nearly all the multimillionaire athletes have complained about how rare it is for journalists covering them to ever take that much time to get their story right. I've often found myself the first person to reveal to them that nearly all the writers covering the sport of boxing aren't getting paid anything for their work. The vast majority of beat writers in boxing work to have a credential to attend and cover fights. They all hold second jobs. And boxing still has enough sway in America to regularly mint the highest-paid athlete in sports, offering up eight figures for an hour's work. As famously hobbled and corrupt as the boxing ecosystem was (boxing was first publicized as "dead" in print in *1898*), any perceived pay-per-view "failure" in that world would eclipse the income produced from an entire generation's worth of chess tournaments and world championships. For better or worse, America doesn't take seriously anything it can't make a buck off of.

Which made my own lack of access to Carlsen and Karjakin with Simon & Schuster's calling card all the more perplexing. The huge push at the match by organizers had been to professionalize chess, reach a broader audience, tap into the popularity of a game played by six hundred million people around the world, and elevate it back to some semblance of the prominence it enjoyed during Fischer's rise. Yet I'd never encountered more impenetrable people to interview than Magnus Carlsen and Sergey Karjakin, presumably the game's greatest ambassadors. I'd been given the impression I'd have had an easier time arranging an audience with Pope Francis at the Vatican. What does it say about the chess world compared to other sports that the finest players are so inaccessible to the general media and the media outside chess that seeks to explore their stories and share them with a wider audience? At least insofar as American perception is concerned, chess is desperate to get out from under the burden of being seen as a sideshow curiosity and reveal its unique virtues and viability as a sport. Yet it still maintains such an intensely tight grip on the enigmatic narratives behind its greatest players, revealing an industry as insecure and paranoid as ever that the glare of more attention could pull back the veil and do more harm than benefit.

In a rare moment of candor, Magnus had confided during his first world championship in 2013 that there were "some demons I keep only to myself." Even going back to Paul Morphy, the "pride and sorrow of chess," and most notably to Bobby Fischer dominating the headlines over Vietnam and Watergate, the mysterious source of creation and violent turbulence at work in the souls of the world's great chess players could rivet the consciousness of their time as much as any event or character. Perhaps because its intrinsic inaccessibility left so much to our imagination. Being ten feet from the world's best chess players, it doesn't take you long to feel like one of those sad, Holden Caulfield–identifying types who drove thousands of miles to Cornish, New Hampshire, to confront

J. D. Salinger at his mailbox, looking to demand some concrete answers.

Despite the allure of spending Thanksgiving on Thirty-Fourth Street watching the Macy's parade or staying home with the family to slice the turkey and watch a few games of football, the attendance at the Fulton Market to watch chess hardly suffered. I, for one, was a lot more interested in the state of how Magnus Carlsen would spend his Thanksgiving after the result of the tenth game of the match following eight draws and being behind in a championship match for the first time in his life. I also wanted to see if Sergey Karjakin, a huge underdog coming into the match, with only three games remaining provided he could hold his lead, could close the show. Coming into the match, Carlsen had won four major tournaments and Karjakin only one—the Candidates Tournament, which had gained him entry to the championship. What had unfolded so far had shocked most experts. Carlsen was running out of time and desperately needed to the settle the score.

Both players began the game nervously, with mistakes made on both sides. Early in the game, Karjakin missed an opportunity to impose a draw with a perpetual check and edge ever closer to victory in the match. Carlsen pushed Karjakin to trade queens on the twenty-fourth move. Carlsen was able to gain a slim advantage over the next ten moves, but a draw still remained the most likely outcome until Karjakin's fifty-sixth move. After hours of Carlsen torturously grinding him down, Karjakin kicked a hornet's nest by moving his rook and aborting any hope of salvaging a draw. Carlsen had been patiently waiting for his opponent to crack while gently but effectively improving his position. Unnoticed by Karjakin, his move pricked a hole in the dike. Nobody on earth was more equipped or delighted than Carlsen to lop off every finger or toe Karjakin tried to use as he auditioned for the part of the Little Dutch Boy, urgently trying to plug the dam. After nineteen more moves, when Karjakin was down to his last toe for a final attempt, Carlsen didn't have to raise his bloody cleaver. Karjakin resigned.

Finally, after another grueling, nearly seven-hour game, on the seventy-fifth move, after thus far sitting down to over two solid *days* of play against Karjakin at the Fulton Market, Magnus Carlsen fought and scratched his way back to his first triumph of the match.

At the press conference, the champion confessed, "It's a huge relief. I haven't won in ten games and that's basically something that hasn't happened to me. It's been a struggle, and it's still going to be a struggle, but at least now we're fighting on level terms."

After Carlsen left the podium, I finally had a chance to bump into Judit Polgár, who had offered commentary for every move of the championship. She reigned as the greatest female chess player in history and broke down more barriers in the biases and prejudices against women in chess than anyone. My mother told me Judit currently occupies a role back in her native country that is analogous to something like the Hungarian Oprah. I tried to catch her off guard by greeting her in Hungarian. A big smile crossed her face at hearing a "hello" in her native language, but when I was unable to maintain a conversation in Hungarian she seemed a little embarrassed on my behalf.

Serena Williams has taken issue with being qualified as the greatest *female* athlete of all time, instead of the greatest *athlete*, full stop. Perhaps she's right. But if you believe chess is a sport—and after all these days at the match, seeing what strain these guys put their bodies and nerves under, cramped in those shitty Staples chairs while trying to concentrate, I absolutely did— Judit Polgár makes a strong case for being ahead of Serena. After all, Williams never competed against the best male tennis stars during the course of her incredible career. From the beginning, Polgár insisted on *only* taking on men. And she beat almost all of them for decades.

FIDE releases a list twelve times a year of every rated player in the world. As of this writing, there are just over 268,000 people on that list. Of those, an anemic 27,000 players are women, a sliver over 10 percent. The world's list of the top one hundred players is entirely absent of any women. Hou Yifan, the current top female player, comes the closest, ranked 105th in the world. Of the 1,550 current chess grandmasters, only 1 percent are women.

Most of the explanations over the years made by top male players to illuminate this skewed dynamic have not only lacked nuance and supporting evidence, but have betrayed a boundless chauvinism in the culture of the game. In case anyone conflated mastery of chess with solid judgment or enlightened wisdom, Dutch grandmaster Jan-Hein Donner offered this gem: "Women have never thought or made anything worth considering." While the English grandmaster Nigel Short, who challenged for the world title in 1993, admitted Donner's quote was outrageously sexist, he conceded that the part about chess had merit. He quoted it in 2015 in an article titled "Vive la Différence!" for the Dutch magazine *New in Chess* before compounding the insufferable sexism with his own take and not altogether persuasive argument: "Rather than fretting about inequality, perhaps we should just gracefully accept it as a fact." Two months later, in a follow-up article for the same publication called "A Beautiful Minefield," he expanded on his reasoning: "While it is difficult, or perhaps impossible, to define exactly which combination of attributes is necessary to become a strong chess player, the existence of fundamentally different cerebral structures between the sexes is, in my view, the ultimate irreducible obstacle to equality in this specific field." He wasn't alone in this endearingly baseless chauvinist view. Garry Kasparov also went to bat on the biological determinist front: "Women by their nature are not exceptional chess players," he said in 1990.

As increasing amounts of academic research undermined such arguments and pointed more toward a glaring participation gap in the genders to explain male domination in chess, Nigel Short shot back in an article claiming the participation argument was "the most absurd theory to gain prominence in recent years. . . . Only a bunch of academics could come up with such a preposterous conclusion." He added in another article from *New in Chess* soon after, "The feminist lobby has become so tyrannical in its shrill orthodoxy, harping on about nurture over nature, sometimes almost to the point of denying the latter."

Women have been competing with men at top chess events since the late 1980s, but the first women's world championship was established by FIDE in 1927. Vera Menchik, born in Moscow in 1906, became the world's first women's chess champion. She held the title for seventeen years, until her death in 1944. On June 27 of that year, Menchik was living with her mother and sister in their South London home during World War II when a German V-1 flying bomb exploded and killed the entire family. The

Women's Chess Olympiad was renamed the Vera Menchik Cup in her honor.

Menchik played a series of games against the top male players in the world during her career, but failed to win a single game against the likes of José Raúl Capablanca, Alexander Alekhine, Mikhail Botvinnik, or Emanuel Lasker. In 1978, Nona Gaprindashvili of Russia became the first woman to earn the title of grandmaster. Maia Chiburdanidze became the second in 1984. And Susan Polgár, Judit's eldest sister, became the third in 1991. Judit Polgár, who retired from competitive chess in 2014, achieved the title of grandmaster the same year as her older sister, only at the age of fifteen years and four months, she beat Bobby Fischer's record as the youngest person ever to do so. From the beginning of her career, Polgár and her father had always insisted on her playing men. The average male grandmaster is rated about 170 points higher than the average female—roughly the gap between the world No. 1 and the world No. 82. No woman is ranked in the world's top one hundred. Judit is the only woman in history to qualify for a world championship tournament against men, which she did in 2005.

Judit Polgár was born in Budapest on July 23, 1976. Polgár, like her older two sisters, was raised by a father who believed geniuses were *made* and not born. Her father, Laszlo Polgár, had not been a chess fanatic prior to the birth of his children; instead he used chess with his daughters as a means to explore his controversial theories particularly because of how conspicuous his daughters' excelling would be against the prevailing chauvinistic wisdom in the game. He believed he could accomplish the same results in any number of subjects, but chess was particularly attractive as it was objective and immediately measurable. Laszlo intensely studied the lives of great intellectuals since his days at university and determined that rigorous study at an exceedingly early age was a common link with all of them. Another theme he identified was "specialization in a particular subject." In 1992, he told the *Washington Post*, "A genius is not born but is educated and trained." He believed any child held the potential for genius.

Despite grave criticism and resistance from the Hungarian government, Laszlo, a psychologist by trade, went about conducting educational experiments to prove the nurture-over-nature argument with his children, with the intensity of Dr. Frankenstein. He believed education must start before children reach the age of three and specialization at age six. The Hungarian government bitterly opposed Laszlo's desire to homeschool his children. Authorities deemed his methods contrary to the socialist ideology of Hungary. They sent in the police and even threatened to institutionalize him. Judit described her upbringing to the *Financial Times* in 2008: "We didn't go to school, which was very unusual at the time. People would say, 'The parents are destroying them, they have to work all day, they have no childhood.' I became defensive, and not very sociable." They were taught several languages and high-level math, but chess was primarily where they invested their energies. "When a child is born healthy, it is a potential genius," Polgár once said. It didn't take long for his methods to demonstrate undeniable results. Laszlo also had the means to hire a team of elite players to assist in the development of his children.

All three of his daughters would become chess prodigies, growing up in an apartment in central Budapest surrounded by thousands of chess books on the shelves. Soon enough, their living quarters were choked further with trophies. Susan began serious study of chess at four and before she turned five, was taken to smoke-filled chess clubs in Budapest and regularly beat accomplished male players. The Polgár family faced intense anti-Semitism as their notoriety grew.

Precisely because chess historically had been dominated by men and many voices in the chess world expressed contempt against the idea women could compete at the highest levels of the game, the Polgár sisters' father rejected any form of discrimination against his daughters competing against men. Laszlo took on the Hungarian Chess Federation, whose rules maintained gender segregation at tournaments. With their eldest daughter, Susan, the Polgárs defiantly challenged the bureaucracy and refused to compete in female-only tournaments. By 1986, Susan was the world's top-rated female chess player. When she wasn't competing, she also began extensively working with her youngest sister, Judit.

The Polgár sisters rose to become extraordinary chess players and, by most accounts I've read, altogether well-adjusted people who led productive lives after their chess careers ended. Susan became a grandmaster at age twenty-two and was the highest ranked female in the world at age seventeen. Sofia, the middle sister, achieved international master status, one grade below grandmaster. But Judit's ambition and achievements set her apart.

She began playing tournaments at the age of six. At twelve, she became the youngest international master in history, two years before either Bobby Fischer or Garry Kasparov achieved the distinction. Former world champion Mikhail Tal publicly remarked that Polgár could become a world champion. That same year, in 1989, at thirteen, Polgár broke into the top one hundred of chess.

During her miraculous climb, many male grandmasters Polgár defeated marveled at the precocious teenager. English grandmaster David Norwood playfully described her as a "cute little auburn-haired monster who crushed you." She was hailed by many insiders as one of the great chess prodigies for the ages. But world champion Garry Kasparov, an abiding sexist, wasn't convinced. He openly referred to Judit as a "trained dog." Another time, Kasparov elucidated the logic behind his assessment: "It's inevitable that nature will work against her and very soon. She has fantastic chess talent but she is after all a woman. It all comes down to the imperfections of the feminine psyche. No woman can sustain a prolonged battle. She will never be a great grandmaster."

But in 1991, soon after Hungary was free of Soviet control, fifteen-year-old Judit got there faster than Kasparov had and for good measure broke Bobby Fischer's record to become the youngest grandmaster in history. In 2002, having lost only ten games over the course of eight years, Polgár defeated Kasparov at a rapid game. It was the first time in chess history a woman had defeated the reigning top-rated player in the world. Where Kasparov had once described Polgár as "talented but not greatly talented," he finally admitted, "The Polgárs showed that there are no inherent limitations to their aptitude—an idea that many male players refused to accept until they had unceremoniously been crushed by a twelve-year-old with a ponytail." In 2005, Polgár was the world's eighth-ranked chess player. This would remain the zenith of her career. By the time of her retirement, she had been the No. 1–ranked female player for an astounding twenty-six years.

• • •

Polgár was too busy at that moment for an extended interview, but she later agreed to answer some questions by phone.

"Coming from such a famous chess family," I said, "with all three of you groomed to be prodigies, what do you attribute your greatness to?"

"It was a combination of things," Polgár said. "I was born into a very special family. Practically by the time I was born, my parents knew that I was going to become a chess champion. I didn't go to school. Both my sisters already played. In the beginning it was very clear that it was my parents. My sisters helped me a lot later on. My character also suited chess. I enjoyed the challenges. The success I enjoyed early on gave me even more motivation."

"What kind of motivation did the chauvinistic culture of chess have on your career?" I asked. "Even the game's best player, Garry Kasparov, repeatedly making such disparaging sexist remarks and so forth."

"It was more motivation than a distraction, absolutely," she said. "Kasparov comes from a background that they don't respect, that they don't believe such things that women are the same level and in mental thinking—I mean, the attitude was the game is for guys. And, to tell you the truth, by results, it was also a fact. So of course there is a big argument and always a huge discussion. I mean, one of the last huge discussions about this gender story was with Nigel Short. I knew Nigel very well. I beat him many times. He could talk about this subject for days. I do believe that I'm an exception up to this point, but I think the only reason is because women don't want to change that and the circumstances are not right. It's not because women are worse. Of course we think differently. Our attitude is different toward success, toward—we're simply different. On the other hand, the higher you are in anything, it's not about gender, it's about personal character. That's what counts. The hunger to win. When you began to play and study."

"There are over 1,550 grandmasters in the world and only thirty-six are women," I said. "How do you perceive your legacy helping to change that disparity?"

"Actually I've heard that all around the world, all of the females who achieved grandmaster status are all still alive. It's changing, but the problem was, in some ways, and it doesn't sound too modest, but I was too good to compare to the others. There was such a huge gap after me that most of the professional women players, whether or not they admired or were inspired by me, still viewed me as an exception."

"And the circumstances of how you and your sisters got involved with chess were extraordinary," I said. "You began very seriously with a hugely ambitious agenda at the age of five?"

"I learned chess almost in the same way I learned my native language," she said. "Chess became a native language to me. It's not just easier to learn languages when you're very young; it becomes as natural as breathing. Some things become that natural to you that that's why you can go into such depth in ways that others can't understand. Many people look at those of us who gave many hours a day to chess and imagine it's boring. That's a very common attitude some people have. How is it possible for chess players to work so many hours? And of course it has its beauty of analyzing, creating, experiencing details, nuances, but then there's winning. And actually Magnus's motivation is not only he likes chess very much, but he likes chess very much because he's winning and he's so hungry for winning. He never stops playing. If he's giving an interview, he's also thinking about chess. It's as natural to him to always have chess going on that it's like breathing.

"Chess for me became a native language. Then it became a game. Later on it became a science and a sport because I had to make a lot of research in order to be successful. I needed a lot of preparation and homework. But while I was researching I found opportunities to create. Creativity was something essential for me. With decades of learning, there is so much memorization of patterns, but also understanding them and how to use them. In many ways, fine chess players are like a chef in a Michelin-starred restaurant. Some people treasure that kind of thing. Others would immediately complain about the small portions! You have to go into the details to be able to treasure and appreciate what we do."

"Many big names in chess history are famous for having snapped," I said. "I wonder if you could explain the pressure you faced mastering chess and then competing at the highest level against other masters."

"I know some people who crack completely after a championship or even getting close to it," Polgár said. "Every game of competitive chess is like an exam. And when we're not taking the exam, we're studying for the exam. We have to get used to that constant pressure. It's one reason I think you have to start young and get used to both the adrenaline and the special state of mind. But people who love to win desperately love the tension. Some people enjoy it with bungee jumping. I would never try that myself. But probably I had some more tense situations in my life than anyone has faced bungee jumping. Sometimes I did feel that I was jumping off from a very high place."

"But Fischer famously said the ultimate pleasure in chess is crushing your opponent's ego," I said. "Watching him squirm. Even more satisfying for him than mating an opponent was them giving up. The sadism of these kinds of remarks is very striking given how much pressure and strain chess players are under."

"That was Bobby's attitude," Polgár said. "I don't think most players share that view."

Polgár saw Fischer's attitude up close. In 1992, a Yugoslavian bank owner agreed to put up the $5 million purse for the Fischer–Spassky rematch. Fischer had been offered millions of dollars to return to competitive chess numerous times since he'd walked away twenty years earlier. Las Vegas offered him serious money to play at Caesars Palace. After bankrolling Muhammad Ali and Joe Frazier with the Thrilla in Manila, President Ferdinand Marcos offered millions for Fischer to return to chess. But when Fischer received a fan letter from an obscure Hungarian chess player named Zita Rajcsanyi and became involved with her soon after, it was Zita's prodding that brought Fischer back into the fold. After Fischer again defeated Spassky in the 1992 rematch in Yugoslavia, he disappeared again and went on the lam as a fugitive from American justice, living out of a hotel room in a quiet Yugoslavian town, right on the Hungarian border.

Judit had been hugely inspired by Fischer's genius at the board and the impact he had on chess. The Polgárs had a family friend who agreed to arrange a secret meeting with Fischer. After another visit, it was the Polgár family who convinced Fischer to move to Budapest, where he remained for several years.

"What was it like meeting him for the first time?" I asked her.

"Of course it was very interesting," she said. "But it was mixed feelings. In some way it was the miracle of meeting your hero. His great victory happened four years before I was born. But when I met him and saw that he was human, it was damaging to the vision I had about Fischer. He was a sick man."

"It was obvious?"

"Well, mentally, with his obsessions about the Russians and the Jews, and about prearranged games and stuff like that. When we invited him to come to Budapest, he was living in a very small place with nobody to talk to."

Finally, I asked her about Magnus—about the pressures he faces.

"I met Magnus when he was very young," she said. "It was very clear that he was a special kid. He was also strange. His father was always with him. They were very close. He was not social at all. He didn't like to talk with people at all really. It was very clear that he was a very closed person. But by now I don't see too much of that. Compared to when he was a kid, he really didn't want to talk to anybody. I am curious to see him have a partner, a wife, and see how that will affect him."

"What did you make of Magnus after he lost the eighth game?" I asked. "When he refused to sit at the press conference and stormed off, from your experience, what was he going through?"

"He cannot stand any emotional moment when he's losing. This is more or less how we feel. And you can imagine that all this happens without talking while you're playing. It's just making moves. Looking at each other. Breathing the same air, which you can always hear. So I mean, without any or hardly too much physical movement or talking, everything is just inside you. And after six hours, either you want to kill yourself or you're in heaven. And sometimes it's one move after six hours. Actually this is what happened to Magnus also. Game eight was nearly seven hours. Even maybe fifteen minutes before the end of that game, he must have thought he could save the game and then, of course, it's just over. It wasn't Magnus having a problem with Karjakin necessarily. It's his anger with himself."

# 11

# FINDING JOSH WAITZKIN

The night before the eleventh game of the World Chess Championships, the headline on the cover of every newspaper on earth
announced that Fidel Castro had died at age ninety in Havana. It
seemed fitting: one of the last legends of the Cold War gone just
as Magnus tries once and for all to cement his reputation as the
greatest player in history and put to rest another Cold War legend,
Bobby Fischer. It also seemed like another sign I was meant to be
covering the championship, similar to receiving my uncle's chessboard in the mail just before I got the assignment. Because most of
what I knew about chess I had learned in Cuba.

On my first visit to Havana, in mid-winter 2000, I met an
antique bookseller on the plane ride over who helped me find
an apartment in a magical neighborhood just off the Plaza de la

Revolución, where Fidel Castro still delivered speeches that occasionally ran for seven hours. A dignified eighty-one-year-old retired doorman stood guard over the street. After leaving his job at the Hotel Nacional de Cuba for one at the newly opened Habana Hilton, he was on duty when Castro and Che Guevara arrived to commandeer the top two floors for their government headquarters. I made friends with all the families on the street. They took me in with more warmth and generosity than did the people in the neighborhood where I grew up. I'd been warned about the poverty in Havana; instead, these people illuminated a poverty of spirit I didn't know I'd faced back home.

I returned to Havana the first chance I got the following year and tried to reconnect with the antique bookseller. He'd told me the only thing that disappointed him about Havana was having to leave it. I found out he'd never had to: cirrhosis had taken his life and he was laid to rest in the Colón Cemetery. When I got back to the street he'd introduced me to, everyone else had left too. The doorman had died and the others had found various means off the island. I asked one of the few people on the block who remained what I should do: *"Resolver,"* he said. To resolve or, colloquially, *get by*. One of the most vital words in the Cuban vocabulary.

I finally found a place in a very different neighborhood: Cayo Hueso in Centro Habana. People in the street led me to a door up the street from a barbershop, a caged-bird store, and a *guaraperia* (crushed-sugarcane-juice stand). I knocked and a latch swung open behind a peephole. A dark burly man with swimming pool–blue eyes unlocked the door and held it open a crack. He had as little English as I had Spanish, so instead of embarking on the usual frustrating pantomime negotiations about the room for rent, he held out two upside-down clenched fists and motioned for me to choose one. This was a ritual he would repeat every time I saw him for the next fifteen years I visited, mostly every other year for longer and longer stretches of time.

I pointed to his left fist, and he opened it to unveil a white knight chess piece. He smirked. *"Bueno. Usted primero."* I had first move. He invited me up onto his padlocked roof (or *azotea*, as Cubans refer to the private rooftops so many retreat to across Havana), where his daughter brought a small mug of coffee, two shot glasses of Havana Club rum, and a beat-up, scratched-to-hell chessboard. His loyal dog, Venus, jumped into his lap and he stroked her fur, and I noticed over his shoulder the most beautiful sunset I had ever seen in my life. I gestured to it and he solemnly pointed to the board before us. It was obvious the view chess offered him was more haunting and lovely than any sunset.

Today this gentleman and his wife rent a room in their Centro Habana neighborhood on Airbnb, but many years before Airbnb was legal in Cuba—and when renting rooms to foreigners was subject to fines and even seizure of property—he provided for his family by renting a room on the roof of a four-story walk-up. So let's call this man Fernando.

Fernando had Chinese, Spanish, African, and German blood, and it seemed to inform all of the features of his face with a noble and almost magical harmony of purpose: getting me to play *one more game.* Chess and Cuba have been inseparable to me ever since. On the streets below us, the slap of dominos was heard well into the night amidst the mingled scents of cigar smoke and diesel fumes, while Fernando and I were invariably playing chess up above.

His chessboard was always waiting on his roof, freshly reset with pieces or, more likely, frozen where a game had been left off. Up there, Fernando also read from one of a dozen books reliving the games of his beloved hero and Cuba's greatest chess champion, José Raúl Capablanca. It was Fernando who introduced me to Capablanca. Forget Bobby Fischer. For Fernando there was only one *gran maestro*—not only on the chessboard, but as an artist, a scientist, a philosopher, even a mystic.

Fernando had a booming voice that dipped into a panicked hush for only two men, Fidel and Capablanca. In all the years I've known him, he's never mentioned Fidel by name. He motions by grabbing an imaginary beard, or simply refers to "Him." Capablanca received the same treatment for entirely different reasons. His genius was metaphyiscal. "Capablanca," Fernando whispered, by way of introduction, "was born in 1888 in Havana to a Spanish army officer. That was the only ordinary thing about him." He held the world championship from 1921 until 1927 and is regarded as one of the great artists of the game. "But he was bigger than the game!" Fernando assured me maniacally. "The *Yuma* at *Time* magazine put him on the cover in 1925! Brinicito, do you know the other men who were on *Time* magazine that year? Winston Churchill! Charlie Chaplin! Leon Trotsky! John D. Rockefeller!" In 1927, *Esquire* declared him the third-most-attractive man in the world. He lost only thirty-five games in his entire professional chess career. When he died in 1942—while watching a chess game in New York's Manhattan Chess Club—his body was sent back to Havana and he was honored with a state funeral.

Chess came to Cuba aboard Columbus's Spanish ships in 1492. And while the shackles of colonialization were broken with

Cuba's revolution in 1959, chess's hold on the island nation has proved considerably more durable. They joke in Cuba that what King Midas was to gold Fidel was to politics, but Fernando always liked to remind me that chess was fifteen hundred years old and would be around long after communism or capitalism. "If a great book never finishes what it has to say, chess is no closer to being solved. But it only gets more beautiful as people try in vain. Just like with life off the board, we all just *resolver.*"

Castro's death made me wonder about the relationship between chess and capitalism—if there was something inherently at odds between them, if that's why no one had ever been able to monetize the game, if that's why the World Chess Championship with its fertilizer and financial management backers was doomed to fail just like every other attempt. It wasn't just that Cuba had always supported chess—though this was true. After Fidel banned professional sports in 1962, huge resources were devoted to making Cuba a global powerhouse in baseball, boxing, and chess. Athletes in these sports were well looked after by the government relative to ordinary Cubans. But baseball players fled to America. Boxers too. Not so much chess players. The promised land of the American dream wasn't anywhere near as easy to cash in with from chess if you escaped.

I once asked Fernando why this was—why today chess is taught in nearly all Cuban elementary and high schools and its universities offer chess degrees while many Americans likely wouldn't know the queen is the most powerful chess piece and not the king. After turning the matter over for a few moments, he put his hand on my shoulder. "We admire *la lucha*," he said. *The struggle.* "Our lives here have always been a struggle, and approaching that struggle with the cunning and intelligence of a chess player is something that commands our respect. The same rules apply on the chessboard as growing up in our crazy system . . . *resolver*."

That's what both Magnus and Sergey were trying to do. *Resolver*. Especially Sergey, considering the tiebreaker format. If the match was still tied after twelve games, then four rapid games would be played. Each player gets twenty-five minutes for all of his moves, plus ten bonus seconds after every move played. If these failed to settle anything, the rules stipulated two blitz games were next. Blitz entails five minutes a side, plus three seconds after each move. If the players are still tied after that, they keep going with blitz until a total of five mini-matches are concluded (ten games in all) to decide the world champion. After that, it could come down to one sudden-death game deliciously known as "Armageddon." The Armageddon "time odds" format has the player who draws the white pieces afforded an extra minute of playing time with five minutes, while the black army begins with only four minutes. If neither army can slay a king, a death sentence is handed down against white and the world title is given to black.

This was the first time Armageddon would be used in a world championship. It seemed another move by the organizers to make the game more exciting for laymen. But it infuriated chess purists, most of whom felt Sergey didn't stand a chance in such a format. Carlsen was the best rapid player on earth and second best at blitz. Karjakin wasn't even in the top ten at blitz.

And so most at the Fulton Market assumed Karjakin would be going for broke in the eleventh game, particularly since he would be beginning the game with white pieces for potentially the last time in the match.

But when Karjakin trotted out the Ruy Lopez opening to start the game, the most classical opening in chess history, which he had employed in seven of the last eleven games, I overheard grumbling in the viewing tent by spectators that he might be exhausted, without much killer instinct left. You could finally feel all the years of computer-based analysis receding from the battlefield and giving way to messy psychology and human emotion.

It was Carlsen, despite playing black, who came out aggressively and looked to have renewed tenacity after having won in the previous game. This wasn't lost on Karjakin, either. Nearing the three-hour mark of the game, Karjakin didn't have much to threaten the champion with. Carlsen pushed a sneaky pawn a little closer toward regal transformation at the end of the board. Karjakin nervously blocked this progress. All paths led to a draw from that point onward. On the thirty-fourth move, after a little more than three hours, both players agreed to accept a draw.

"Of course the pressure is much higher here," Karjakin said at the press conference, to explain his caution during the game. "You understand that any mistake can basically be the last one. . . . The pressure here is another story from other tournaments."

Carlsen smiled broadly when he was told over two hundred of his countrymen in Norway had stayed up to watch him play. He was asked if he felt any added pressure at this point in the match:

"Today I was a lot calmer than I was in the last few games. I'm optimistic about the rest."

●　　●　　●

It was that same afternoon that I saw Josh Waitzkin, the kid whose story had been the basis for the film *Searching for Bobby Fischer*, which had been based on a book by Waitzkin's father, Fred. I loved the book, but I've always had trouble with the fundamental dishonesty of the film. In a lot of ways it is a highly deceitful recruitment poster for chess and chess prodigies, with its falsely reassuring impression of a father's attempt to nurture his prodigiously talented son and have him fitted for some ruby-red slippers in which to mosey on down Bobby Fischer's yellow brick road. I especially despised the Bobby Fischer presented in the film: a Disney-fied hero with an incorruptible purity of soul defending America against the Soviets with a Cold War backdrop even more paper-thin than that of *Rocky IV*. Fischer himself never saw the film, bitterly complained about how it was an invasion of privacy, and hated having his name exploited to help sell it.

The true story, of course, was much messier, not only for Fischer but for Josh Waitzkin. In the introduction to his 2007 book *The Art of Learning*, Waitzkin talks about how his father's book and later the movie had led to a crisis for him both personally and as a chess player where his game "began to unravel." His newfound celebrity status had overwhelmed him. During a rare interview he gave, in a 2014 podcast with Tim Ferriss, he claimed paparazzi had followed him everywhere after the film's release and that he was "living in a spotlight in a way I wasn't prepared for." Waitzkin soon left not just New York but the continent to escape the pressures he felt. He would later emerge as a highly successful martial artist, even winning a world title in tai chi push hands. Based on the research I'd done, he'd mostly steered clear of the media since returning to New York.

Waitzkin would turn forty in just a few months, but there was still something essentially boyish about his face. He was there with his old coach Bruce Pandolfini, who was played by Ben Kingsley (who had won an Academy Award for portraying Gandhi) in the film. I approached them and asked Josh if he had any interest in sitting down to talk. His guard went up and he perfunctorily offered his email address. I knew immediately I would never hear from him again, but wrote him anyway. I respected that he had said what he had to say and written what he had to write about his own experiences and didn't feel any urge to share anything more.

But I thought I still might learn something from talking to his father—something that might shed some insight on the relationship between Magnus and Henrik. I reached out to Pandolfini. He generously vouched for me, and Fred Waitzkin invited me over to his office in Midtown to talk.

After a horrible ordeal at the dentist having work done, he completely forgot about our meeting and I was wandering around his office building harassing his wife on the phone trying to figure out what was going on. We met a couple hours later in his office, and while Waitzkin's mouth was still bothering him, he made some tea. I immediately felt at ease around him. Waitzkin is in his early seventies and has a combination of warmth and directness about him that makes you feel as if you and he have known one another for years. He had just finished writing a preface and afterword for a new edition of *Searching for Bobby Fischer* that was to be published soon.

In the fall of 1984, Fred Waitzkin met with a Random House editor to explore the possibility of writing his first book, about, of all things, chess in the United States. Waitzkin was fascinated by how so many talented people could abandon comfortable lives, conventional careers, even marriages to essentially live in squalor and devote themselves to chess. At the end of the meeting, Waitzkin mentioned offhandedly that his young son Josh had recently begun playing. He was very good. The bigger surprise was how Fred, a sportswriter by trade, had more fun watching chess than anything he was covering professionally. That's when his editor fell silent and declared, "Your book should be focused on Josh."

The central dilemma for Fred Waitzkin was not being sure that his seven-year-old son truly was a chess player. Who knew if he would stick with it even *tomorrow*, let alone make chess his life's path. What if he wasn't especially gifted even if he did? If Josh decided to give up chess immediately after Fred took the advance to write the book, what then? Even if Josh stuck with the game, would anyone care about his story? Feeling both "elated and stricken," Fred accepted the challenge. "So began the most unlikely adventure that changed my life and my wife's life, greatly influenced my son's life, and, indeed, launched the chess lives of tens of thousands of kids across the country and even around the world."

Already when Josh took to the tables at Washington Square Park, Fred heard the whispers of "young Fischer" from other players. Soon both father and son were hooked. Josh was a natural talent who worked hard to get even better. As his son began to regularly win tournaments, Fred confessed he felt as though he was also winning and that the two were becoming "like we were one being." One afternoon, while leaving a local chess club with Josh, Fred was accosted by an aging female regular. "So you're here again with your little boy," she said. "Dragging him into this smoke-filled place to play chess. Don't you know you're making him into an addict? You are just trying to make up for all the things you couldn't do with your own life." This commentary hit home and gave Fred profound pause. In his book's new introduction, he claims the words of this old woman have followed him ever since. But instead of abandoning the project, he included his growing ambivalence as a thread in the book's evolving narrative.

Fred invited his son to read *Searching for Bobby Fischer* for the first time in twenty years and include his impressions in the new edition's afterword. Josh found it an immensely emotional experience. He confesses to having grown up with a deep sense of conditional love. But looking back at the story as a forty-year-old man, his perspective had changed. "My demons became our demons. That's what you wrote about." With two children of his own, Josh has struggled with the desire to re-create the bond he felt with his father, despite nursing the earlier impression that his father was a narcissist offering love conditional on his son's success. Josh admits to having struggled with the strength of their bond while growing up but finds himself wounded by its absence now that he's grown up. But at some point, the choice to walk away from competitive chess became clear. "There was a moment I realized I didn't want to spend my life staring at sixty-four squares as a metaphor for life," Josh told his father. "I wanted to look at life directly."

"What got you hooked on chess in the first place?" I asked Fred.

"It's just so intense," he said. "It just sucks you in. Josh's chess life really began at Washington Square Park. We were basically living there. He would play speed chess for hours. That was the world. Who was there, objectively speaking? Chess hustlers, drug addicts, high school dropouts, lawyers who had given up the law, chess masters who didn't have twelve dollars in their pocket. But that was the world to us. Such an intense world. For me of course there was so much projection involved. Because my son was— I didn't understand where it came from, this ability to be so good, so young. He was beating all my friends. We had been playing for ten or fifteen years. He crushed me before he was seven. I thought I was hot stuff at chess. He crushed me. And even vicariously, it sucked me in with watching Josh. I began to feel chess was what was really important in life.."

"What if Josh had become Magnus Carlsen?"

Waitzkin covered his face with his hands to smother his discomfort.

"That probably would have killed me. He probably saved my life."

"Tell me about watching it end with Josh."

"I don't remember one conversation. He decided to stop before I was comfortable with it. We weren't fighting, but my motor was still going while his was slowing down. It wasn't making him happy. He was lonely at tournaments. He wasn't excited playing anymore. After the movie there was a lot of resentment toward him in the chess world. The attention he was getting. He showed up at tournaments to sign one of his chess books and there'd be a line outside three blocks long, when Kasparov, who was there, didn't have twenty-five people waiting for his autograph. He became very self-conscious with all the attention."

"The last section of the book isn't so much about Josh *becoming* Bobby Fischer as about you trying to track him down."

"I didn't look as hard as I might have." Waitzkin smiled. "I was afraid if I found him I would hate him so much that it would ruin my whole metaphor. So I kind of looked for him and didn't at the same time when I was out in California. It was such a goof, because when I was writing about it nobody else was at that point. And I discovered he was doing all these crazy things. Taking out his teeth and walking in disguises and all the crazy people he knew. Now it's all cliché Fischer stuff. It wasn't then. Like Salinger after *Catcher in the Rye*, Fischer became mythically important but the attention made it impossible for him to proceed. Success and celebrity didn't do that to Kasparov. Carlsen seems as if he's suffering under some of that pressure."

"Can I ask you something?" I asked.

"Sure."

"In the epilogue to *Searching for Bobby Fischer*, you leave Josh with readers on a very promising note scoring a draw against Kasparov when he's only eleven. The symmetry with Magnus as a boy doing the same thing against Kasparov is eerie. *60 Minutes* showed footage of Kasparov really not handling it all that well. Both your son and Magnus were burdened by so many of the expectations of assuming the role of Bobby Fischer after those games against Kasparov. But Magnus went on from his draw with Kasparov to become the highest-rated player ever and a world champion. That didn't happen for Josh. You describe being lured in and losing yourself along the path of realizing your son's talent as a prodigy. There were some dark consequences for both of you. Now Josh doesn't really play chess anymore. He really doesn't want to talk about chess anymore either. But Magnus sitting on top of the mountain really doesn't want to talk either. When he lost in the eighth game to Karjakin, the effects were chilling to watch up close. Like a nervous breakdown in slow motion. It reminded me a bit of Kasparov's response after losing to Deep Blue."

"Kasparov told me children shouldn't be doing this the way children like Magnus and Josh and himself did this as little boys. Josh has told me he couldn't imagine sending his own son, who is five years old, into the playing halls I sent him into. That pressure he was under playing national championships at seven? He couldn't imagine that for his own son. He doesn't want to. Kasparov told me himself it just takes too much out of you."

When on the morning of the twelfth and final game I watched the players enter the soundproof cage from the viewing tent, it felt as though Charles I's executioner stood poised with his axe aloft over the maple-and-rosewood chessboard, ready to bring it down against the necks of both players' kings, while Karjakin and Carlsen were each left with one last chance to seize the rope and bring down the guillotine's blade.

The event organizers had looked to capitalize on the do-or-die atmosphere with their customary brand of cynical obliviousness and had jacked up admission prices so high that the final regulation game was preposterously the least attended of the match. It made the atmosphere all the spookier at the Fulton Market, like that of an auction house where hardly anybody had even bothered to show up for the masterpiece up for sale.

Maybe it was for the best. Fans who couldn't afford $200 to attend were likely soothed when they soon learned they had missed not just the briefest but possibly the most pedestrian game ever played in the history of championship chess. Thirty moves in thirty-five minutes. The board looked like a Quentin

Tarantino movie, with nearly every important piece quickly and indiscriminately massacred. With only their bishops left standing surrounded by a cabal of ineffectual pawns, both players agreed to the tenth draw of the championship.

Many had expected Carlsen to use this game as an opportunity to solidify his place in the pantheon of chess masters with an inspired if not transcendent performance. Instead, Magnus decided on his better odds in a tiebreaker situation. Instead of Mozart we got elevator music. Karjakin's lack of aggression was perplexing. Why exactly was he eager to draw? Was he really more comfortable in a tiebreaker situation? Carlsen was no slouch if you sped up the time.

The play had inspired a chorus of moans from nearly everyone watching. British grandmaster Nigel Short said of the game, "If the twelfth game were a restaurant dish, I would send it back to the chef."

A fan standing next to me put it in terms a little more suited to New York: "Fuck that shit. I just paid two hundred bucks and took a day off of work for thirty-five minutes' worth of that bumper-car bullshit chess?"

Spectators' faces brightened after organizers announced post draw that anyone holding a ticket to this abysmal game would gain free admission to the tiebreakers. But Sergey was looking less relieved.

"Let's hope there won't be Armageddon," Karjakin nervously said at the postgame press conference.

# 12

# 50.Qh6+!!

Wednesday, November 30, was the final day of the championship. It was also Magnus Carlsen's twenty-sixth birthday. With sudden death's accelerated play and claustrophobically limited amounts of time, this version of Carlsen and Karjakin's duel would be messier, each step even more treacherous and unforgiving. It would expose their hearts as much as their minds, as this kind of chess was inescapably more reliant on primal instincts than careful preparation.

Again, the chess purists hated it—hated that after more than three deliberate, painstaking weeks a championship should be decided in such a crude fashion. It was the same argument soccer purists have against the World Cup being decided by a shootout. But most everyone I spoke to relished that the title should be decided by the world's top two chess players essentially engaged in a game of intellectual hot potato with a make-believe grenade.

If chess were a religion, its adherents would make it the fourth largest in existence. And even under the frigid drizzle falling from a pigeon shit–gray sky, a mob of hundreds of the faith's most fervent acolytes—hordes of wide-eyed, adorable chess nerd kids among them—formed an hour before the doors opened, their bated breath floating visibly in the air. Meanwhile, around the corner, at the VIP entrance, a swath of 1 percenters arrived and were instantly let in, ready to sink their fangs into the lifeblood of the game and suck out its vitality for useful photos to hang on the wall at business meetings.

The tailored suits and elegantly clad women showing off their jewelry thrust on the event the unwanted feeling of a museum gala. You couldn't smell chess's thick aroma for all the expensive perfume. Suddenly it felt like I was back at the Plaza Hotel on opening night of the championship, before Carlsen and Karjakin's games had scraped off all the polish and let chess breathe again. It just made way too much sense that the honorary first move of sudden death was to be made by Peter Thiel. Silicon Valley billionaire. Donald Trump advisor. Ann Coulter confidant ("My biggest hero other than Trump," she once said). Hulk Hogan–*Gawker* lawsuit bankroller. And, apparently, former chess prodigy who at the time was ranked 962 in the US and 21,930 internationally.

Organizers had announced that more than ten million people from around the world were watching the event live over the internet. Norway television was broadcasting the game in prime time. When I got up to the VIP room and negotiated my way through the flutter of European and Russian accents hanging over the martinis and hors d'oeuvre trays, I tossed my notebook and jacket down on my usual couch one last time next to Frank Brady. He was serenely staring out the window at the Brooklyn Bridge moping under the sad, overcast sky. Brady smiled.

"Perfect chess weather outside, don't you think?" he said.

I overheard someone saying that Vladimir Putin's press secretary, Dmitry Peskov, had arrived. Just then I noticed a roped-off section of the room nearby that appeared to be a *double* VIP room, with two stiff, utterly paranoid-looking, imposing men standing guard, and extra-exclusive catered food laid out. Cynic though I was, I had to admit: the mini-tacos looked delicious.

In the corner, I noticed Thiel's face, which in repose resembles that of a particularly disgruntled electric eel. He was sitting at a board. And who was across from him? Oh yes, the creepy Scandinavian grandmaster I had met on the first day. He had all the social graces of spam email made flesh, someone who had spent three weeks at the match feverishly soliciting endless phone numbers, business cards, and email addresses for possible future business dealings. And now, on the last day of the match, he'd hit pay dirt! A guy whose estimated worth was higher than some countries' GDP! The pair looked good together.

Incredibly, Thiel wasn't even the richest guy in the room. That was Russian venture capitalist Yuri Milner, who had roughly $3.7 billion to Thiel's $2.5 billion.

Just as I noticed him, one of the bodyguards came over and said not to stand so close to the rope. Then there was a commotion behind me, and the bodyguard seemed to reach, ever so briefly, Jason Bourne–like, for something sinister under an armpit. Until he saw it was a five-year-old girl running back to her dad.

Obviously, the world chess championship was a prime location for would-be child assassins of technocrat overlords.

I kept watching Thiel and the Scandinavian hustler, wondering at what moment he would offer his business card and ask Thiel for his contact info. He waited too long. Soon, Thiel was approached by the organizers and told that it was time for him to make the ceremonial first move. As he quickly stood up and left the table, the Scandinavian looked heartbroken.

At two o'clock, the players entered the executioner's room as photographers took their final images. Liberated from the grind of interminable games, Carlsen seemed energized—he looked menacingly poised and relaxed. Carlsen came out fast. After thirty minutes and twenty moves, he was ahead on the clock by more than ten minutes over Karjakin. Carlsen then continued to impose pressure on Karjakin, and that pressure consumed increasingly more time. Yet after thirty-seven moves over fifty-five minutes, another draw was accepted.

Ten minutes later the second game began. Both players had removed their jackets. Carlsen, with white pieces, as he had in game five, opened with the Giuoco Piano. Karjakin continued to fall behind on time as Carlsen turned on the pressure and gained material. After forty minutes of play, with less than two minutes of time on his clock, Karjakin was being fitted for a straitjacket on the board. Queens were traded on the thirty-seventh move. As the positions on the board lost complexity, Carlsen relaxed further until he looked like a man on a breezy stroll in the park. Meanwhile Karjakin was down to forty seconds.

A rush of excitement went through the crowd when the computer engines shown on the flat-screens all over the venue determined a mate was available to Carlsen—but it was far too many moves away from his current position. Unfortunately, Carlsen unwittingly eliminated that path by moving his bishop instead of his king. In the last stretch, Carlsen had one last opportunity to mount a lethal attack but moved the wrong bishop on the seventy-third move. As the final seconds on Karjakin's clock evaporated, with only four seconds left, somehow Karjakin miraculously found the space to make the drawing move. After eighty-four moves, the game ended in a stalemate.

The spectator gallery roared approval. Judit Polgár declared from her commentator's booth that Carlsen had thrown away the match. Carlsen folded his arms and stared at the board despondently.

Just before the third game began, as Karjakin adjusted his back-row white pieces, Carlsen released and refolded his arms again, closed his eyes, and proceeded to collapse against his headrest in disgust with himself. I heard gasps around me as if this might signal that the pressure was too overwhelming and that soon, as had happened in the eighth game, he might crack. After the eighth game he'd had nearly a day and a half to recover from the overwhelming disappointment. Here, now, after squandering a commanding position in the previous tie break, he had ten minutes.

Yet just before the arbiter circled the table and triggered the clock's time into motion, Carlsen opened his eyes and stared at the board, and something new arrived. Those deep-set brown eyes suddenly came alive in a way I hadn't seen before. He looked angry. But it wasn't a helpless anger. It was a determined anger. Ruthless even.

In the first few minutes, the pieces danced over the board. The harmony and beauty of their movements seemed more like ballet than like the standard chess metaphor for war. Then Karjakin uncharacteristically went on the attack. Perhaps after living on the edge for so much of the previous game, he was determined to remove the clock factor. Maybe he wanted to pounce on Carlsen's frustration from the last game and exploit any emotional fragility that lingered with so little time for him to recover from the errors that cost him his victory. Maybe he'd gained the necessary confidence to go for the win from his ability to escape defeat against the world champion. Just as I was watching Karjakin leaning tensely over the table pondering his next move, Judit Polgár's commentary echoed through the venue: "I want Sergey, *if* he's going to be the champion, I want him to *crush* in one game. You can't just be playing defensive. Please. If he wants to take the crown, he has to show that he goes for it and attacks Magnus and does it all the way that he wins the game. He *beats* Magnus. Because until this point, Sergey was defensive and when Magnus lost, it was a mistake of Magnus. It was not the great creative play by Sergey. He was genius in his defense."

I turned to have a closer look at Carlsen. It's a lot easier to theorize about human behavior than it is to just look at it. Over the course of the next few minutes, as I watched Carlsen contend with this definitive moment in his career, I became aware that on some level he finally seemed to embrace, rather than look cursed and burdened by, the role he had spent his life carving out for himself in the world. He looked ready to make the role his own.

Instead of using his army of pieces in a methodically coordinated maneuver against his opponent, you could feel real emotion. With the slowly increasing pressure Carlsen relentlessly applied on Karjakin, something profoundly changed for me. There was some kind of metamorphosis where as a spectator, instead of feeling my customary awe at his arresting powers of calculation or grueling levels of concentration, I now felt connected to his heart in a way I'd only experienced with artists. The anger and tension left him and he was no longer just trying to break Karjakin, to cave him in and witness the final gasp of the collapse. He was somewhere else. Far away. Alone. The entire world and everyone who ever played this game could be looking over his shoulder, but Carlsen seemed to remember in these strange moments that he could find the answer before anyone else.

If Karjakin could Houdini his way out of any bolted safe dropped into the river, Carlsen added a new element to the trick: with menacing fluidity, he lit a fire under the tank to bring the water to a slow boil. Karjakin floated over the endless possibilities within each steaming bubble while time ebbed and dwindled away.

After the twenty-second move, Karjakin was on a precarious ledge, driven there by time. Six moves later, with Carlsen bearing down, Karjakin was down to three minutes on his clock.

Karjakin frantically searched for an escape, some means to reverse the script of where the game was heading. He glanced with despair over at his clock and saw Carlsen's relative *eternity* of seven minutes remaining versus his own twenty seconds.

In the final moments, as Carlsen had his queen and rook dug into an attacking position well into enemy territory, Karjakin desperately pondered his position one last time and moved a rook. He had thirteen seconds. On the thirty-eighth move, Carlsen briskly slid his rook down to Karjakin's back row, malevolently poised to steal a bishop and place a bow on the game. As his time ran out Karjakin gazed over the wreckage of a lost battlefield and extended his hand across the board, offering his resignation. Cheers erupted all over the Fulton Market in recognition of the quality of the game.

Karjakin now needed a win to survive, or Carlsen would win the championship.

Karjakin started with the Sicilian Defense, and the audience sarcastically applauded—*finally* something besides the Ruy Lopez. Instead of a defensive crouch, Karjakin offered a fighting stance. Carlsen rested his chin in the palm of his hand, and I found myself uncontrollably smiling in the darkness of the viewing tent as time stood still.

With survival looming only on the increment—gaining ten seconds on the clock after each move—Karjakin was forced to risk more than he ever had to stay alive in the match. A draw would no longer work. He needed a win. And to deliver a win, he needed a miracle. Yet as he strove to create, Carlsen's will resisted any interference toward his objective. The clock bled down and there were whispers around me that Karjakin might be luring Carlsen to go for a win in the hopes of exposing more chances for a mistake. I looked around the venue and spotted a little girl of maybe three alone at a chessboard, so consumed with the board and pieces she'd forgotten about the championship. Carlsen only needed a draw to retain his crown, but it was clear he wanted something more.

As Karjakin's time eroded to only thirty seconds, he feverishly looked to prolong what the engines and experts were all predicting looked nearly inevitable. Before the forty-ninth move of the six-teenth game of the match, Carlsen took twenty-nine seconds to identify and savor his gift to chess history.

It's deeply troubling to contemplate how often we fail to recognize the important moments in our lives until much later, when we're helpless to do anything about them. Yet the worse tragedy might be when we *do* recognize those moments as they arrive and intuit exactly the precise ways in which they will irrevocably define us to ourselves and shape the rest of our lives. It is here, despite doing our best to seize these moments, that we risk betraying, at the core, how terribly miscast we feel in the roles of our lives while simply attempting to play ourselves.

But Magnus Carlsen recognized the moment and became even more alive and present. As he looked at the board, he saw it. Nobody else did. Not Sergey across the table or Judit Polgár in the commentators' booth or Henrik Carlsen or any of us who stood on the other side of the glass watching. We had absolutely no idea. But Magnus did. He had fought all his life to earn an indelible moment on the world's stage, performing for history. After he'd squandered numerous opportunities and nearly lost the match, everything he had worked for, everything he was or ever imagined himself to be, now stood on the precipice, hanging with his title and the horrible consequence of who this curious creature might be in the world without it.

Carlsen slid his rook deep into enemy territory to place Karjakin's king in check.

Karjakin quickly fled with his king to h7.

Carlsen slid his queen to the h6 square, entrapping and setting up the scaffolding for a king's execution.

The notation "50.Qh6+!!" deconstructed means this: Carlsen's queen moved to the h6 square and placed Karjakin's king in check, illustrated by the plus sign. The exceedingly rare double exclamation marks are awarded not only for a move of sublime majesty on the board but also for the element of unexpectedness in the creation. The closest equivalent I can think of arises in bullfighting, where even the most legendary matadors might go an entire career without facing a bull of such exceeding virtue an audience of thousands wave handkerchiefs to demand a pardon. Before Carlsen's queen sacrifice to win the crown in New York City, the most famous double exclamation mark awarded for one happened sixty years earlier and two miles away in Greenwich Village, at the Marshall Chess Club, on October 17, 1956. On the seventeenth move, a thirteen-year-old Bobby Fischer played "Be6!!" against twenty-six-year-old Donald Byrne in "The Game of the Century" and electrified the chess world. Moves worthy of double exclamation marks almost never happen between players competing at the highest levels of the game, yet Carlsen had achieved his with a mind-blowing coda at a world championship against one of the best players on earth.

This was the most magical moment of the match. Chess had always been a forbidden garden behind the eyes of all its greatest composers. For fifteen hundred years they had thrown flowers down a bottomless well. But during those twenty-nine seconds, without the world knowing it, Magnus Carlsen had turned the key and trespassed through a gate to his most private garden in order to gather a bouquet of roses to place on Karjakin's grave.

Even for a few seconds after it happened, no one saw it. It was that good. That magical. There was a prolonged moment of deafening, paralyzing silence. And then total fucking pandemonium.

Children squealed and even casual spectators threw up their hands in disbelief. I watched as those grandmasters and older men and women who had devoted their entire lives to this game struggle to break free from the overwhelming incredulity at what they had just witnessed. They were overcome with anguished beauty.

Karjakin gave one parting glance at the infinite possibilities of chess reduced to only one remaining inescapable outcome: which of Carlsen's rooks would he hire to assassinate his king?

"50.Qh6+!!" was instantly recognized by aficionados as one of the most riveting codas in the history of the World Chess Championship. Carlsen had warned a reporter at the postgame press conference from a previous game that if they were looking for art, "you will have to look elsewhere." He proved himself wrong with the most convincing case at the most vital moment offered in all of chess. As long as chess is played, the move will be studied by chess historians. And they will be as helpless as scholars attempting to unriddle the power of the last line in Rainer Maria Rilke's "Archaic Torso of Apollo": "You must change your life."

As I made my way through the crowd in the VIP room to get to the press room, I could hear a chorus of "Happy Birthday" being sung to Carlsen.

Then I saw Frank Brady, paralyzed with awe on the couch, staring at the board on a flat-screen TV, his mouth still gaping.

As I approached, he couldn't break away from the board on the screen.

"*How* did he find . . . *that*?" he gasped. "Gorgeous."

On my way home from the championship, to decompress a little, I walked the two and a half miles north to the hustlers' tables at

Washington Square Park to watch some games. There, I over-heard a father and his daughter ask one of the players where the Chess Forum was. I followed them over to Thompson Street and looked through the store window as they were greeted by Imad Khachan inside. Then I got lost in the boards on display in the storefront window, a cross-section of nearly two millen-nia of world history distilled into hundreds of new and antique chess sets, showing the game's journey across fifteen hundred years and well over a billion players' lives, irrespective of culture or creed: boards based on King Arthur, on Nigerian village life hand-carved from scraps of wood, the Vatican warring against mercenaries, China's Qing dynasty defending its territory, the Crusades attempts to annex the Holy Land, hand-painted pieces of Columbus's crew staring down Native Americans, American and British troops from the American War of Independence standing guard, the bluecoats and grays of the American Civil War doing battle over slavery, boards based on the battle of Pearl Harbor and other epic contests of World War II.

And then history had brought the horrors of 9/11 to the Chess Forum's door. Bobby Fischer was fifty-eight and cheering on the devastation from Japan. Magnus Carlsen was ten years old and likely in his bedroom in Norway practicing. Donald Trump was in his New York penthouse calling into a local TV station and boast-ing that one of his buildings near the site was once again the tallest in downtown. Now it was fifteen years later and Bobby Fischer was dead and Donald Trump was president and Magnus Carlsen was champion of the world.

As I stood there on Thompson Street, I thought about the three questions my editor had wanted me to investigate. The first—why isn't Magnus Carlsen more of a household name?—I could have answered without the benefit of the last three weeks. As a rule, our track record with appreciating genius in its own time has proved very limited. Galileo. Van Gogh. Kafka. Poe. Dickinson. But this is itself the answer to the second question: What is the secret to Carlsen's greatness?

I don't pretend to suggest the art communicated from sixty-four squares of an ancient board game meaningfully translates with any of the scope or immediacy of music, paint on a canvas, or words on a page. But that is precisely the point. It is very likely that Magnus Carlsen brings as rare a talent to his craft as Beethoven or Van Gogh brought to theirs, and he approaches his craft with equal devotion *despite* how inaccessible that craft remains to the world. *That* is the secret to his greatness: that it remains a secret.

Then there was the final question, the one that I had become most preoccupied with over the course of the assignment: Will Magnus Carlsen be able to avoid the unhinged fate of Fischer and Paul Morphy and Peter Winston and so many others?

And at that moment, I remembered another time I had been standing on a street corner. It was years ago, outside the Plaza de Toros de las Ventas in Madrid. I had never seen a bullfight before and wasn't sure I even wanted to. I wasn't sure I wanted to go inside. So I asked a group of aficionados standing outside the front entrance what separated the greatest matadors in Spain listed on a nearby poster. They offered the names and motioned with their hands to indicate how close the various matadors allowed the horn to pass to the matadors' hearts with each charge.

But they left out one name on the list: José Tomás.

"Him?" I asked, pointing at Tomás's name. "How close does he let the horn come?"

They all looked embarrassed before one explained, sheepishly, that Spain had never seen its greatest living genius perform his most sublime works of art. The horn came too close. Nobody watching could look through their hands. Even men who worshiped the dark beauty of the *corrida* were simply too afraid to peek.

No great matador was ever considered so without coming within an inch of his life from a goring and then returning with renewed willingness to risk it all again. If he couldn't come back, he couldn't be taken seriously as great. So it should be with all great artists. They are burdened with the expectation of accepting more danger than inferior practitioners, of allowing the horn ever closer to their hearts.

And if they fail? If they are fatally gored? The popular narrative is that winners show their character and strength in finding a way to win, while losers are weak and lack the necessary mettle. Yet winning is a single note—pure in tone but alone. It's the losers who are confronted with who they really are and find depth and perspective as a direct consequence of failure. They take us far closer to human truths when we hear their stories compared to those of their vanquishers. Winners are rarely self-aware. Losers have no choice. The fundamental, irrevocable lesson of life and nature is loss. Winning is a temporal illusion.

What would Fischer have been without madness? What will Carlsen be? A personality grows—or doesn't grow—before some feeling of worthlessness. It is a hole that is never filled. A breeze always comes out of it. The two standard responses of life tend either to be in succumbing to it or overcompensating. Nothing can wipe away that essential void, but for a time, perhaps, it can be occupied by something else and the world can be overcome, its towers falling in silence, its pieces erased from the square.

All these quests are in the end the issues of children. Underneath springs an innocent yet awesome desire to conquer all, an unchecked power. Only a child would dream of becoming world heavyweight champion, of becoming president, ruling the world, or the world in miniature, conquering a chessboard, devoting a life to a game so few truly understand.

What that power has developed around it is a defense mechanism. Against growing up. Against time. And I suppose here is where the whole issue dovetails not just with art but with all human achievement. A well-balanced adult, as the model is presented to us, should never attempt these things. The gamble is too great, the risk too enormous, the failure too final. Because to lose . . . to lose turns it all into nothing but a lesson, a transient thing in a transient world. Perhaps that is why, even when we don't understand, we celebrate above all others those who dare to take that risk.

Somehow they do it for everyone.

# THE THREE KINGS OF COLOGNE